Above and below: Baby Bunting, page 88. *Right:* Angora V-Neck With Floating Sleeves, page 78.

Left: Yellow, Blue, and Magenta Crocheted Cardigan, page 68. *Above:* Green, Tan, and Yellow V-Neck, page 58. *Below left to right:* Heavy Red Jacket, page 49; Yellow, Blue and Magenta Crocheted Cardigan, page 68; Red, White, and Brown Tweed Cardigan, page 36.

Above: Heavy Black and White Turtleneck, page 64; Hefty Black Cardigan With Hood, page 52. *Below, left:* Five-Color Sweater With Crocheted Body and Knit Sleeves, page 44; *right:* Yellow, Cream, and Brown Sweater, page 56. *Right:* Sunshine Cape, page 66.

Left to right: Simple Fisherman's Sweater, page 90; A Poncho Even a Kid Could Knit, page 94; Crochet Jungle, page 85.

Olive and Rust Shawl Collar Cardigan, page 46.   Flower Sweater, page 24.

Above left: Red and White Rayon Evening Jacket, page 82; Linen Boat Neck Pullover, page 30. *Above right:* Sweater with Cowboy, page 34; Windmill Sweater, page 42. *Below, left to right:* Raspberry Mohair Pullover, page 32; Three Grays and Red Sweater, page 40; Rose-Colored Bumpy Stitch Pullover, page 62.

Above: Detail from Hooded Turtleneck With Gloves Knit On, page 71. *Below:* Kid's Cowboy Jacket, page 92; Hooded Turtleneck With Gloves Knit On, page 71.

Left to right: Textured Cotton V-Neck, page 20; Gray Crew Neck, page 60; Navy Linen Vest, page 22; Shell Stitch Crocheted Linen Cardigan, page 26.

Ribbon Cap Sleeve V-Neck, page 80.

Cinnamon Shell, page 18.

Kid's Cowboy Jacket, page 92; Big Purple Sweater, page 54.

Rainbow Sweater, page 74.

Left: Cotton Beach Jacket, page 28; *right:* Multicolored Pastel Cardigan With Ridges, page 38.

THE
SWEATER
BOOK

Judith Glassman

35 original sweater patterns for men, women, and children

quick fox

NEW YORK LONDON

*To all the women in my family, with special love
and gratitude to my mother, Beatrice Berman;
my grandmother, Edith Gadell; my Great-Aunt
Anna Bentz; my Aunt Shirley Klein; and my sister
Arlene Bellefond. And with many thanks to the
knitters and crocheters who worked so tirelessly
and with such enthusiasm—Shirley Klein, Yvonne
Malyack, Chris Dominiani, and Dorothy Provost.
A special thank you to Barbara Littell, who trans-
lated my patterns into all sizes.*

Also by Judith Glassman

New York Guide to Craft Supplies
National Guide to Craft Supplies
Step-by-Step Beadcraft

Copyright © Judith Glassman, 1976
All rights reserved.

International Standard Book Number: 0-8256-3061-4
Library of Congress Catalog Card Number: 76-8069
Printed in the United States of America.

No part of this book may be reproduced or transmitted in any form
or by any means, electronic or mechanical, including photocopying,
without permission in writing from the publisher: Quick Fox,
33 West 60 Street, New York 10023.

In Great Britain: Book Sales Ltd., 78 Newman Street,
London W1, England.
In Canada: Gage Trade Publishing, P. O. Box 5000,
164 Commander Blvd., Agincourt, Ontario M1S 3C7.

Book and cover design by Jean Callan King/Visuality
Illustrations by Lily Hou
Photographs by Herbert Wise and David Frazier

CONTENTS

A SECTION OF COLOR PHOTOGRAPHS
APPEARS AT THE FRONT OF THE BOOK.

PREFACE

I learned to knit when I was in a cast. Not one of your small arm casts, but a full-fledged body monster which encased me from my shoulders to my hips. The cast (known affectionately as my cast of thousands) was designed to immobilize my humerus, snapped smartly at the elbow in an automobile accident. There I was for six weeks, trapped with my good right arm held immobile at shoulder level, elbow slightly bent. I looked as if I was permanently raising an imaginary glass to my lips.

Looking back on it now, I can vaguely understand why I taught myself to knit then. I couldn't get around very well; reading, always my salvation in times of reduced activity, was as difficult to manage as anything else; and perhaps, at some unvoiced level, I felt that learning to knit would help my bones to knit.

Whatever the reason, knitting came to me in my early twenties, which was late, considering that my family is full of knitters and crocheters and that opportunities to learn were always all around me. My Great-Aunt Ann, for example, for many years owned a yarn store in Ossining, New York. She turned out dozens of fabulous dresses and sweaters. When I was working on this book, my father showed some home movies of the family, taken when I was a little girl. In one of them the camera pans from one of my aunts to another. Each of them is busily clicking needles, inching forward on yet another sweater. The mainstays of my childhood winter wardrobes were the heavy pullovers and cardigans knit for me by my mother and grandmother.

Sweater-making has been a family affair in many periods throughout history. At its peak in England in the sixteenth through mid-nineteenth centuries, sweater-making was a major industry, done by mothers and their children with yarns spun from the wool of their own sheep. Elizabeth I, realizing the value of this industry, refused to grant William Lee a patent monopoly on his knitting machine, developed in 1589, because she felt such a machine would pose a grave threat to the income of her cottage workers. Later events proved the canny

queen was right, as the machine, when finally improved by William Cotton in the 1860s, took over the bulk of sweater production with astonishing rapidity, leading to the swift decline of hand-knitting as a profitable pursuit.

It is impossible to know what was the first sweater. There is speculation that it could have been Joseph's coat of many colors or even Christ's robe, which is described as a garment that could not be cut. Whatever it was, one imagines that the first wearers of sweaters were grateful for their warmth, perhaps not realizing it was the minute holes between the stitches that trapped body heat so effectively.

Sweaters have not varied much throughout the centuries. If a sweater strays too much beyond a certain shape, it is no longer a sweater. It is a coat or a shawl. If it is not knit or crocheted it is a jacket or a shirt, and the crafts of knitting and crocheting impose still another set of limitations. But within these limits we can find a range of shapes and surfaces. There are the heavily embossed oiled wool fishermen's sweaters of the Aran Islands, worked by sailors with a richness of cables, bobbles, and twist and seed stitches. There are sweaters from Fair Isle, decorated with colorful patterned bands. There are the misty lace of sweaters from the Shetland Isles, the surface geometrics of Scandinavian sweaters, the people and animals that appear on German and Dutch sweaters, the mysterious symbolism of South American and Mexican sweaters, and, of course, the straightforward utility of that American classic, the tennis sweater.

An exciting trend is the exuberant sweaters being turned out by a group of sophisticated craftspeople who are knitting and crocheting works of art that are colorful, complex, and only incidentally wearable. These new explorations of the medium are truly inspired.

Today, with the handwork explosion of the 1960s still expanding, and with sweaters so fashionable once again, knitting and crocheting are everywhere. Sweaters are advanced to completion on trains,

HOW TO MAKE A SWEATER

planes, subways, buses, in doctors' and dentists' waiting rooms. Yarn fills the hands and the click of knitting needles is heard above the din of traffic.

The sweaters in this book include many basic styles, adaptations of old forms, some new forms, and a lot of ideas and suggestions that can be adapted and used. Beginning sweater makers may wonder at the scarcity of plain, unpatterned sweaters in this book. I feel that plain sweaters can easily be bought. Why bother to make one? If you like the shape of a sweater and are afraid to try a patterned stitch, or a combination of colors, of course you can make a swatch in a plain stitch, figure your gauge (see page 11), and work out your sweater so it's plain and simple. Novices should look for the sweaters marked easy. Once you've gotten through an easy sweater you can attempt a pattern marked medium. After a medium sweater you're on your own. I hope this book leads to hours of pleasurable handwork and years of useful sweaters.

If you've never knit or crocheted before, you're liable to find it awkward at first. Stick with it. It will probably only take an hour or so of some concentration before you're comfortable with knitting needles or a crochet hook.

Before I begin to detail instructions, one word of warning. The most common mistake beginners make is to knit or crochet too tightly. I remember the first sweater I made, back in my cast. I wanted so desperately to make my stitches even that I pulled every stitch as tight as I could. Each stitch was a minor skirmish, a row was an exhausting experience, and the finished sweater was as dense and heavy as a rug. Don't worry about evenness of stitches at the very beginning. Just get the knack of forming them, and regularity will come as you work.

KNITTING

Casting On: Casting on is the way to get the required number of stitches on your knitting needle. To cast on at the beginning of a piece, first make a

slip knot in your yarn, far enough from the tail end so you have about an inch for each stitch. Hold the knitting needle in your right hand and slide the loop of the slip knot onto the needle. Wrap the tail end of the yarn over your left thumb and the ball end over your left index finger, holding the needle between them (a). *Insert the point of the needle

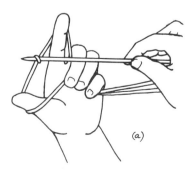

(a)

under the yarn which is wrapped around the thumb, forming a loop. Then place the point of the needle over the strand that comes from the index finger (arrow, b), and using the point of the needle, pull that strand through the loop (c), slip the loop from your thumb, and close the stitch by pulling down against the tail end of yarn with your thumb.* Repeat between the *s. Don't make the cast-on row too tight or you'll have trouble working the first row.

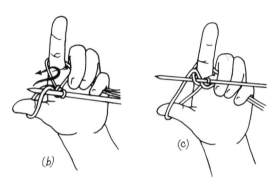

(b)   (c)

Knit: Hold the needle with the stitches in your left hand, the yarn looped around the left forefinger.

Hold the empty needle in your right hand. Insert the right-hand needle into the first stitch on the left-hand needle, from front to back. Catch the yarn that's coming from around your left forefinger under the right-hand needle, from back to front (arrow), and pull this yarn through the stitch. This

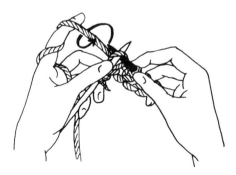

makes one stitch on the right-hand needle. Let the old stitch drop off the left-hand needle and you are

now in position to make the next stitch in the same way.

Garter Stitch: If you knit every row, you are doing what is called the garter stitch, a flat stitch which is good for borders. The garter stitch looks like this.

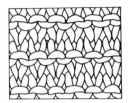

Purl: Hold the needle with the stitches in your left hand, yarn looped over your left forefinger, the empty needle in your right hand, the same as for knitting. Insert the right-hand needle into the front of the stitch from right to left. Pass the yarn over the top of the right-hand needle, from front to back, then back under the needle, toward you (a).

(a)

Draw the needle with the loop you've just formed through the stitch on the left-hand needle. Slip the new stitch to the right-hand needle, allowing the old stitch to slip off (b).

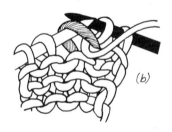

(b)

Stockinette Stitch: If you knit one row and purl one row, you are doing the stockinette stitch, one of the most common knit/purl combinations. The knit side of your work will look like this (a). The purl side of your work will look like this (b). In

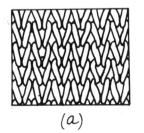

(a)

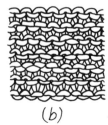

(b)

other words, when the knit side is facing you, you knit; when the purl side is facing you, you purl.

Ribbing: This is a knit/purl combination that is frequently used for cuffs, sweater bottoms, and necklines because it pulls together and holds these edges snugly. It is done by knitting one stitch and purling the next across one row. In subsequent rows, you knit over the stitches that were purled in the previous row and purl over the stitches that were knit. On an even number of stitches the pattern for knit one, purl one ribbing looks like this: Row 1: K 1, p 1. This row is repeated for the desired number of inches. On an odd number of stitches, the pattern is: Row 1: K 1, *p 1, k 1, repeat from *. Row 2: P 1, k 1, end p 1. Knit two, purl two ribbing is also effective, but ribbing with more than two stitches won't pull in enough.

Seed Stitch: Just about number one on my all-time hit parade of knit/purl combinations, the seed stitch is also a knit one, purl one combination, but this stitch broadens out, doesn't curl, and has a wonderfully bumpy texture. You do this one by knitting over the stitches that were knit in the previous row and purling over the stitches that were purled. On an even number of stitches the seed stitch pattern is written this way: Row 1: K 1, p 1. Row 2: P 1, k 1. On an odd number of stitches, the pattern is: Row 1: K 1, *p 1, k 1, repeat from *. Row 2: K 1, p 1, end k 1.

You will not have to remember this consciously for very long. After a couple of rows of ribbing or seed stitch you'll recognize what has to be done where just by looking at your work, and you won't need instructions at all.

Slip Stitch: Slip a stitch from the left-hand needle to the right-hand needle without working it. The yarn is carried in front of the work (the side facing toward you, whether or not that is the actual front), or in the back of the work (the side facing away from you, whether or not that is the actual back). Slip stitches are used for surface decoration, or to carry a color up through several rows, as explained in Colors, page 13.

Yarn Over: Used for an open, lacy effect or to increase (see below). Pass the yarn over the top of the needle, from front to back.

Increase: To make a piece of knitting wider you must add stitches, or increase. A common way to do this is to knit or purl into the front and back of the same stitch. Or make an extra loop on the needle, with a yarn over.

Decrease: You decrease or eliminate stitches in order to narrow a piece of knitting. Knit or purl two stitches together. There are other ways of increasing and decreasing for special effects. These are explained in any sweater pattern where they're required.

Buttonholes: For the first row of a buttonhole, bind off (see below) the required number of stitches. On the return row, cast on the same number of stitches, as follows: Loop the yarn around the left thumb (a). Insert the needle upward in front of the thumb, through a loop (b). Slip this loop onto the needle.

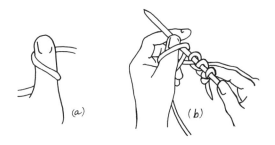

Binding Off: To finish off a piece of knitting so it won't unravel. Work two stitches in the pattern stitch. Insert the point of the left-hand needle into the first stitch made, as shown, and slip it over the

second stitch made. Being careful to hold the second stitch on the needle, let the first stitch drop off. Work one more stitch. In the same way as before, pass the first stitch on the right-hand needle over the new stitch, and let the first stitch drop off, being careful to hold the second stitch on the needle. Continue in this way until only one stitch remains on the right-hand needle. Slide the stitch off the needle, cut the yarn, and draw it through the last stitch.

Special Equipment:
A *cable needle* is a small J-shaped needle to which stitches are slipped so that they can be crossed over other stitches to make cables.

A *stitch holder* looks like a giant safety pin and is used to hold stitches that are to be picked up later. It is most often used for the center stitches at a neckline.

A *circular needle* is used for seamless or tube knitting or when there are too many stitches to fit on straight needles. Circular needles come in several different lengths. Use the right length needle for the job at hand. A 29-inch needle, for example, will not work for a 14-inch tube.

Double-pointed needles are sold in sets of four and are used, as circular needles are sometimes used, for making seamless circular garments or to pick up stitches around a neckline. Stitches are divided evenly among three needles and are knitted off with the free fourth needle.

A *yarn needle* with a big eye is used to sew knit or crocheted garments together.

Picking Up Stitches: In sweater patterns for crew necks and some V-necks you'll be instructed to pick up stitches around the neckline after the sweater is sewn together. On a crew neck you do this by holding the sweater, right side out, with the front facing you. Use four double-pointed needles. Insert the knitting needles into the stitches as follows: the first along the left side of the neck, starting at the back of the neck, from back to front; the second picks up the neck stitches at the front of the neck, which will generally be on a holder, from left to right. With the third pick up the stitches along the right side of the neck, from the front to the back of the neck. Knit these stitches for the required distance. Work a V-neck the same way, except work the left side of the neck first, and when that is finished, work the right side. This will give you a neat ribbed overlap in front.

To finish a turtleneck, pick up all the stitches around the neck, starting at the center back, with either a circular needle or a set of four double-pointed needles. Work as directed. This will make a seamless turtleneck. To bind off using circular needles, pretend the circular needle is a straight needle and use a straight needle as the other needle. You can't bind off on the two ends of the circular needle alone. Take my word for it.

Dropped Stitches: At some point in your knitting career you are bound to let a stitch slip off the needle and slide down a few rows. It will create a laddered effect and can be pulled up again with a crochet hook, as follows. To pull up a dropped stitch on the knit side of a fabric: With the dropped stitch in front of the ladder, insert crochet hook through the stitch from front to back, under first ladder thread above stitch. Hook ladder thread through stitch. Repeat until you have pulled stitch all the way up. Slip stitch back onto knitting needle. To pull up a dropped stitch on the purl side of a fabric: With the dropped stitch behind the ladder, insert crochet hook through the stitch from back

to front, then under first ladder thread above stitch. Hook ladder thread through stitch. Repeat until you have pulled stitch all the way up. Slip stitch back onto knitting needle.

CROCHETING

Chain: The chain starts your work. It serves the same function as casting on in knitting. Hold the crochet hook any way that's comfortable for you. I've always held mine as though it were a pencil.

To start the chain, make a slip knot, pull the knot open so it forms a loop, and slip this loop onto the crochet hook. Close the loop by pulling the ball end of the yarn. Now loop the ball end of the yarn around your left forefinger and hold the tail end of yarn between the thumb and third finger of your left hand (a). Put the ball end over the hook (b).

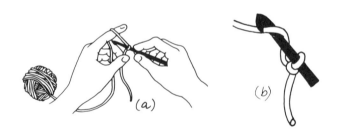

Start sliding the hook back through the loop. Let the hook catch the yarn over and continue with the same motion until the loop has passed over the hook, with the yarn caught in it (c). Repeat this action for each chain stitch. (Remember to keep those stitches loose.)

Single Crochet: Chain 15. Insert the hook into the second chain from the hook (a). Bring the yarn

(a)

over the top of the hook and pull the hook down, just as you did to chain, pulling the hook through one loop. You now have two loops on the shaft of the crochet hook (b). Put the yarn over the hook

(b)

and pull through two loops (c, d). Continue making

(c)

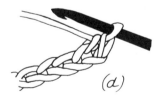

(d)

single crochet stitches in the same manner until you've reached the end of the row (e).

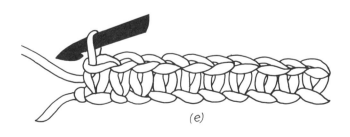

(e)

Chain one and turn the work. Your first row of single crochet will look like this.

Make the first stitch of the second row in the second stitch after the turning chain (arrow, above). Begin this stitch by inserting the hook under the two top threads of the stitch in the previous row. Work to the end of the row, inserting

your hook for the last stitch into the turning cnain at the end of the previous row (arrow, below).

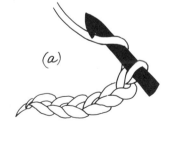

Half Double Crochet: Chain 15. Put the yarn over the hook (a). Insert hook into the third stitch from the hook and put the yarn over the hook again (b).

(a)

(b)

Pull through one loop (the chain stitch). There are now three loops on the hook. Put the yarn over the hook again (c) and pull it through all three loops.

When you get to the end of the row your work will look like this.

Chain two (d), turn your work, and begin the next row, inserting your hook into the second stitch from the chain two, picking up both loops of that stitch.

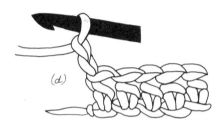

Work to the end of the row, working your last stitch into the turning chains of the previous row.

Double Crochet: Chain 15. Put the yarn over the hook and push the hook through the fourth chain stitch from the hook. Put the yarn over the hook and pull through the chain stitch as for half double crochet. There are now three loops on the hook. Put the yarn over the hook and pull through two loops, leaving two loops on the hook (a). Put the yarn over the hook and pull through these last

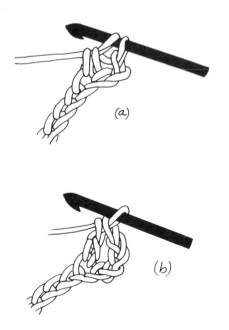

two loops (b). Continue working in this manner until you reach the end of the row. Chain two to turn. Your first row of double crochet will look like this.

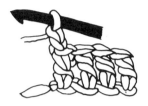

Work the first stitch of the next row in the second stitch after the two chains; work the last stitch in the turning chains.

Slip Stitch: Chain 15. Insert hook into the second chain from hook, yarn over hook and pull through both loops at the same time. Continue until you reach the end of the row. Chain one to turn.

Increase: Work two stitches in one stitch. To increase a large number of stitches, chain the required number of extra stitches at the end of the row.

Decrease: You can decrease in several ways. If a crochet pattern says simply "decrease," work two stitches as one. The technique varies slightly according to the stitch you're using.

For single crochet, work a single crochet until there are two loops on the hook. Insert hook into the next stitch and start a second single crochet, working that until there are three loops on the hook. Yarn over and pull through all three loops.

For half double crochet, work a half double crochet until there are three loops on the hook. Yarn over and insert hook into the next stitch and work until there are five loops on the hook. Yarn over and pull through all five loops.

For double crochet, work a double crochet until there are two loops on the hook. Yarn over, insert hook into the next stitch and begin a second double crochet. Work until there are four loops left, yarn over and pull through the two loops. Yarn over and pull through three loops.

You can also decrease at the beginning of a row by slip stitching over the required number of stitches and then starting your regular stitch. Or you can decrease the required number of stitches at the end of a row by leaving them, that is, not working them at all.

Ending Off: To end off, simply pass the yarn end through the last loop and pull taut.

Buttons: You can crochet your own very funky buttons (see p. 2 of color section for photos of sweaters with crocheted buttons) this way. Chain three stitches. Join the first stitch to the last stitch with a slip stitch. Round 1: Single crochet six stitches into the ring. Round 2: Single crochet two stitches into each stitch. Round 3: Single crochet one stitch into each stitch. Round 4: Single crochet, skipping every other stitch. Round 5: Single crochet, skipping every other stitch. Stuff the cup with yarn. Round 6: Slip stitch across the top, closing cup. Knot and stuff end into cup.

ATTACHING NEW YARN

When you run out of yarn, simply attach the end of the old ball to the end of the new ball with a knot. Most instruction books suggest you attach a new ball of yarn at the end of a row. I don't find it makes any difference. If you pull the ends through to the wrong side of the work and catch them in as you knit or crochet the next few stitches, the knot will not show.

MARKING ROWS AND STITCHES

Mark a row by tying a piece of yarn in a contrasting color around the first stitch in the row. In knitting, mark a stitch or a place in a row by tying a piece of yarn in a contrasting color around the needle between that stitch and the next. The marker stays on the needle as you work and reminds you to perform whatever operation is necessary. In crocheting, you will have to mark the stitch and keep moving the marker from row to row. You can buy little plastic stitch markers in any five and ten, but I have never used them.

STITCH GAUGE

Stitch gauge is the number of stitches to the inch and the number of rows to the inch you get when you knit or crochet. A stitch gauge is given at the beginning of every knit or crochet pattern. It will determine the size of your finished garment. It is a *vital* indicator, and working to the wrong gauge can mean disaster in terms of fit.

Let's say a pattern calls for six stitches to the inch. Being enormously eager to wear that sweater right away, you start on the back, without knitting or crocheting a little sample swatch. Perhaps, instead of working six stitches to the inch, you're actually working five stitches to the inch. What's one measly stitch per inch, you ask? Well, one stitch per inch over a distance of twelve inches adds up to twelve stitches. At five stitches per inch that's almost two and a half inches. If you work the front of the sweater the same way, that adds on another two and a half inches, or just about five extra inches of sweater. There are very few sweaters where fit is so uncritical that an extra five inches won't make a difference. Gauge, I say again, gauge. And if it seems that I'm overstating, it's only because of my own bitter experiences with sweaters that turned out . . . well . . . wrong.

Taking a gauge is simple. Cast on or chain 20 stitches in the yarn you're going to use, on the suggested needles or hook. Work about four inches in the pattern stitch. (As you can see, making a sample to check gauge also gives you an opportunity to become familiar with any complicated pattern.) Bind off and block lightly. (See Blocking, page 12.) Lay the swatch down on a flat surface and carefully measure the number of stitches and the number of rows in an inch. Take a couple of measurements at various places on the swatch. If your swatch has too many stitches to the inch, try needles or a hook one size larger; if you're getting too few stitches to the inch, try needles or a hook one size smaller. After a couple of sweaters you'll know whether you knit larger or smaller than the suggested gauge, and you'll probably start out with the right size needles or hook.

Now that you're convinced you won't be wasting time making swatches, here are some suggestions on how to use swatches so you don't waste yarn. First, you can always just rip a swatch out when you've finished measuring and use that yarn in your sweater. Even better, you can label it with the type of yarn, stitch instructions (if the stitch is a fancy one), and needle size. String your swatches together or staple them into a notebook, and you'll have a valuable record for future projects. By playing around with such a collection you can come up with sweater designs of your own, using combinations of various patterns. Or save your swatches in a big box and put them together to make an afghan, a bedspread, a wall hanging, place mats, a rug, a sweater, dress, suit lining, and so on. You can make your swatches all the same size or all different sizes and plan a pattern that will fit them all together. I loved making swatches for the sweaters in this book because it gave me a chance to experiment with different yarns and different stitches.

And, after all is said and done, you know how long it takes to make a swatch? Maybe fifteen minutes—if the stitch is complicated.

BLOCKING

I never could understand why blocking isn't called pressing, which is essentially what it is. It will flatten stitches that curl and will give your garment a finished look. There are few knit stitches that really *need* blocking: the stockinette stitch is one. Most textured knit stitches and most crochet patterns don't need it at all. You *will* want to block if a sweater has gotten really creased as you carry it around in your knitting bag, or if you think a little judicious blocking might stretch a piece that's too small. (See Mistakes, this page.)

Sweaters are traditionally made in several pieces: a back, front (or two front halves if the sweater is a cardigan), and two sleeves. Block each piece separately before the sweater is sewn together. Outline the desired measurements of a piece and pin it to a padded surface (a folded-up sheet is perfect) with rust-proof pins, coaxing it to fit the outline. Cover the piece with a pressing cloth (any piece of smooth, heavy fabric) and steam. Press down with the iron on one spot, lift it up and move it to another. Don't slide the iron around the sweater, and *never block ribbing*. Check for the blocking information in each pattern instruction.

PUTTING SWEATERS TOGETHER

Complete each sweater by first joining the back to the front, then closing the sleeve seams, then attaching the caps of the sleeves to the body armholes.

Sewing Seams: For knit sweaters the most professional seams are made with the back stitch. Pin the seams together so the right sides of the sweater pieces face each other. Thread a yarn needle with a

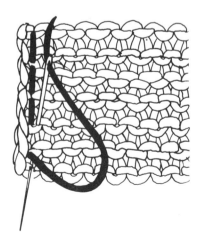

yard or so of yarn. Tie a knot or make a couple of stitches in the same place to secure the end. Backstitch through the stitches right next to the edge. Don't pull your stitches too tight or you'll have a puckered edge.

To sew crocheted sweaters together, use an overhand stitch.

Weaving Edges Together: Use this technique when joining knit stitches that have been left on holders, instead of bound-off edges. Slip half the stitches to one needle. Thread a yarn needle with a length of the yarn. Starting at one edge, pass the yarn through the first stitch on one needle, then through the first stitch on the second needle. Next, pass the yarn through the next stitch on the second needle, then through the second stitch on the first needle. Continue in this manner, always working in the same direction, until all stitches are joined.

Conceal yarn ends by catching them in as you sew your seam, or by hooking them under a few stitches with a crochet hook.

MISTAKES

What is worse than trying on a handmade sweater and finding that it's too big? Trying one on and finding that it's too small. *That's* an experience that separates the weak from the strong. Happily, all is usually not lost. There are a number of techniques you can use to save your sweater besides the masochistic solution (ripping the whole thing out and starting over again) or the martyred one (giving it to someone thinner). If you merely want the sweater you've been seeing in your mind's eye to fit *you*, try the following.

If your sweater is a little too tight, outline the pieces to the correct size and block them pinned to that outline. If it's much too small, figure out how much has to be added where. Take out the seams and knit or crochet strips to fit in between pieces of the sweater. You can make these pieces nearly invisible by matching the pattern of the rest of the sweater, or you can experiment with different textures and colors. You can add strips in the same way to a sweater that's too short or a neckline that's too low. Crocheting a couple of rows around neck or bottom edge will sometimes work here also, depending on the sweater pattern.

A too-short sweater with a ribbed or stockinette bottom can be lengthened this way: open the side seams, cut a thread in one of the last stitches near the bottom of the sweater and pull the thread. All the rows below this thread will fall off. Pick up the stitches with a small knitting needle and reknit with needles of the correct size in ribbing or stockinette stitch.

If a sweater is too long, you can hem it, or use the same seam-opening and thread-cutting technique, cutting off the excess plus the ribbing. Pick up the stitches and reknit the ribbing. If the sweater is too wide, make big seams, machine stitch a double or triple row of zigzag stitch near the seam, and cut away the excess.

See page 8 for dropped stitches.

COLORS AND PICTURES

There are several ways you can use more than one color in sweaters. The simplest is to make rows of different colors. Work one row in color A, cut the yarn, attach color B, work one row in color B, cut the yarn, attach color C, work one row in color C and so on. Or work two rows in one color, two rows in another, or three rows in one color, eight in another, four in one, six in another—anything.

An excellent way to create color patterns in knitting that look complicated but are fairly simple is to use the slip stitch method, where a color can be carried above its row by slipping it instead of working it. The slipped stitch is worked on the following row, or even the row above that. You can see that the slipped stitches will be elongated. With slip stitches you generally work two rows in a color and never have to cut yarns or change color in the middle of a row. To get a neat edge, bring the new color up from behind the old one, and remember if you're slipping more than a couple of stitches to keep the unused thread running loosely behind the work. Once you get the rhythm of slipping any particular pattern you'll find it goes much more quickly than regular knitting—when you slip a stitch you don't have to work it, so of course it's faster.

A third method of working with color is the Fair Isle method, where you change yarn every time there is a color change. This method is the most versatile; you're not limited by having to be careful not to slip too many stitches at once. You can really paint with yarn and create any sort of fantasy you can imagine. The only drawback is the possibility of tangled yarns when you're working with a lot of different colors, and you can reduce this possibility by working with short lengths of yarn wrapped around and tucked into slit pieces of cardboard that act as small spools. Remember to wrap your yarns around each other whenever you change colors. If you don't, your work will be holey.

DUPLICATE STITCH

Different colors can also be introduced by embroidering on the finished sweater, using the duplicate stitch. You can embroider in the same weight yarn or yarns of different weights, creating different textures as well as pictures.

If you, like me, have never been able to draw, you may despair of ever creating a picture on a sweater—or on anything, for that matter. One thing I've discovered is that you don't have to be able to draw to create pictures. All you have to know is how to trace. Trace any picture—as complicated as your ambition allows—onto graph paper, then adapt it to knitting or crocheting by making the lines or areas of the drawing correspond exactly to the boxes of the graph. Mark each graph box with a symbol you have selected for that color. You will wind up with a graphed pattern of your picture. All you need to do is knit or crochet, placing the colors where indicated on the graph. Or make the sweater plain and embroider the picture on the sweater, again following the colors on the graph.

THE YARNS IN THIS BOOK

ABBREVIATIONS AND SYMBOLS

I admit to a certain reactionary fascination with rayon, but other than that it's natural fibers all the way for me. Almost every sweater in this book was made of wool, linen, or cotton, of the 100 percent pure variety. The baby bunting is synthetic. It's practical to be able to throw a baby bunting in the washing machine. Also, wherever I asked about wool for baby clothes I was told in a horrified voice that infants were often allergic to wool, and what kind of unnatural woman was I, anyway? I'd never heard of infant's wool allergy before. Perhaps it's really mother's allergy to high cleaning bills, but that at least is rational and understandable.

For classic American yarns I used those of the country's largest suppliers: Spinnerin, Bucilla, Reynolds, Lily Mills, Coats and Clark's. The rest of the yarns I used are imports or are manufactured by smaller companies: Tahki, Mexiskeins, Golden Fleece, Joseph Galler, Fibre Yarn, Berga/Ullman, Frederick J. Fawcett. If any of their products are hard to find in your area, write to them. (See Suppliers, page 17.) Although I highly recommend all of the yarns I used, if you want to use others for any reason, you can substitute any yarn that will give the required gauge. Wherever a change of yarn will make a major difference in the way a sweater looks or feels, I'll say so.

Very often a sweater calls for a fraction of a skein more or less for each larger or smaller size. You won't be able to buy a half skein of any yarn, so you may have some yarn left over. Generally the extra amount won't be costly, and extra yarn can always be used for hats, scarves, children's sweaters, potholders, rugs, crewel embroidery, belts, purses, socks, bedspreads, and on and on. Lots of substantial scraps can add up to colorful, imaginative combinations. (Of course, you have to remember that I'm a fiber freak, and having extra yarn gives me a feeling of security. If you really have nothing to do with leftover yarn, you can always send it to me.)

Knitting and crocheting instructions look cryptic if you're not used to them, but the abbreviations and symbols are an effective shorthand.

If a series of stitches is enclosed in parentheses, that combination of stitches is to be repeated. The number of repeats is given right after the parentheses. For example, "(yo, k 2 tog) 3 times" means: work a yarn over, knit two stitches together; do it again; and do it a third time, before going on to the next stitch in the pattern.

Stitch patterns are written once for the whole row. For example, "Row 1: K 1, p 1" means that you alternate knit and purl stitches across the entire first row. Sometimes the instructions for a row will read this way: "Row 1: K 1, *p 1, k 1, repeat from *, end k 1." This means that you knit the first stitch, then purl one, knit one to the end of the row. After the last purl/knit combination there will be one stitch left over, which should be knit.

Abbreviations

beg	beginning	p	purl
ch	chain	sc	single crochet
dc	double crochet	sl st	slip stitch
dec	decrease	st	stitch
d-p	double-pointed	sts	stitches
hdc	half double crochet	tog	together
inc	increase	yo	yarn over
k	knit		

SIZES

Women's Sizes	Small (8—10)	Medium (12—14)	Large (16—18)
Bust	34	38	42
Waist	24½	27	31
Hip	34	38	42
Shoulder Back	12½	14	15½
Armhole Depth	7½	8	8½
Sleeve Width	12	13	14
Sleeve Length	18	18½	19
Wrist	8¼	8½	8¾

Men's Sizes	Small (36—38)	Medium (40—42)	Large (44—46)
Chest	38	42	46
Shoulder Back	15	16½	18
Armhole Depth	8½	9	9½
Sleeve Width	15	16	17
Sleeve Length	18½	19	19½
Wrist	9	9¼	9½

Children's Sizes	Small (4—6)	Medium (8—10)	Large (12—14)
Chest	25	28	32
Shoulder Back	10¼	11¼	12¾
Armhole Depth	4¾	5	6¼
Sleeve Width	9¼	10¼	11¼
Sleeve Length	11	13	14
Wrist	6½	6¾	7

Baby Sizes	Small (1)	Medium (2)	Large (3)
Chest	20	21	22
Shoulder Back	9	9¼	9½
Armhole Depth	3¾	4	4¼
Sleeve Width	7½	8	8½
Sleeve Length	7½	8½	9½
Wrist	5	5½	6

SUPPLIERS

Countless thanks to all of them for their cooperation. Write to them if you cannot find their yarns in your area. Those marked with * do a retail mail order business. The others will direct you to the nearest retail outlet.

Bucilla (Bernhard Ullmann)
30-20 Thompson Avenue
Long Island City, New York 11101

Spinnerin
30 Wesley Street
South Hackensack, New Jersey 07606

Golden Fleece*
P.O. Box 1142
Radio City Station
New York, N.Y. 10019

Tahki*
336 West End Avenue
New York, N.Y. 10023

Frederick J. Fawcett*
129 South Street
Boston, Massachusetts 02111

Fibre Yarn*
840 Sixth Avenue
New York, N.Y. 10001

Berga/Ullman*
P.O. Box 918
59 Demond Avenue
North Adams, Massachusetts 01247

Mexiskeins*
P.O. Box 1624
Missoula, Montana 59801

Joseph Galler, Inc.
156 Fifth Avenue
New York, N.Y. 10010

Lily Mills Company*
Shelby, North Carolina 28150

Coats and Clark's
17-01 Pollitt Drive
Fair Lawn, New Jersey

Reynolds Yarns, Inc.
230 Fifth Avenue
New York, N.Y. 10010

SELECTED BIBLIOGRAPHY

There are many other good knitting and crocheting books in addition to the ones I've listed here. These, however, are the ones I turn to most often.

Brock, Delia, and Bodger, Lorraine. *The Adventurous Crocheter.* New York: Simon and Schuster, 1972.
Duncan, Ida Riley. *The Complete Book of Progressive Knitting.* New York: Liveright, 1968.
Thomas, Mary. *Mary Thomas's Knitting Book.* New York: Dover Publications, 1972.
Walker, Barbara G. *A Treasury of Knitting Patterns.* New York: Charles Scribner's Sons, 1968.
——. *A Second Treasury of Knitting Patterns.* New York: Charles Scribner's Sons, 1970.

CINNAMON SHELL

LIGHTWEIGHT SWEATERS • EASY

This shell is easy and cheap to make and fun to wear. It can be worn by itself as a summer top, or over a shirt as a vest.

Sizes: Women's small (medium—large).

Materials: Coats and Clark's Speed-Cro-Sheen, Cinnamon, 4 (4½—5) spools. Knitting needles, #4. Steel crochet hook, #0.

Gauge: 6 stitches = 1″; 9 rows = 1″.

Pattern (multiple of 8 stitches): Rows 1, 5, and 9: K 6, yo, k 2 tog. **Row 2 and all even rows:** P. Rows 3, 7, 11: K 7, *k 2 tog, yo, k 6, repeat from *, end k 1. **Rows 13, 17, 21:** K 3, *yo, k 2 tog, k 6, repeat from *, end k 5. **Rows 15, 19, 23:** K 4, *k 2 tog, yo, k 6, repeat from *, end k 4. Garter stitch.

A PHOTOGRAPH OF THE CINNAMON SHELL APPEARS ON THE NEXT-TO-LAST PAGE OF THE COLOR SECTION.

BACK: Cast on 80 (84—90) sts. Work 8 rows in garter st. To establish pattern, **Row 1**: Work in pattern to last 0 (4—2) sts, k 0 (4—2). Continuing in pattern, inc 1 st each end every fourth (third—third) row 11 (15—18) times—102 (114—126) sts. Work even until piece measures 7″ (7″—7½″). Work 8 rows in garter st. Bind off.

FRONT: Work same as back.

STRAPS: Cast on 12 sts. Work even in garter st until strap measures 15″ (16″—17″). Bind off.

FINISHING: Block sweater pieces. Sew front and back together. Sew straps to front and back. With right side facing, work 1 row sc along edges of straps.

TEXTURED COTTON V-NECK

LIGHTWEIGHT SWEATERS • EASY

The deep ribs on this handsome sweater give it a highly embossed look. The stitch is really elementary, and the finished product is smashing.

Sizes: Women's small (medium—large).

Materials: Lily Double Quick Crochet Cotton, Cream 9 (10—11) skeins. Knitting needles, #4. Steel crochet hook, #0.

Gauge: 6½ stitches = 1″; 8 rows = 1″.

Pattern (multiple of 3 stitches plus 2): Row 1: K. Row 2: P 2, *k 1 in the back of the stitch, p 2, repeat from *.

A PHOTOGRAPH OF THE TEXTURED COTTON V-NECK APPEARS ON THE NEXT-TO-LAST PAGE OF THE COLOR SECTION.

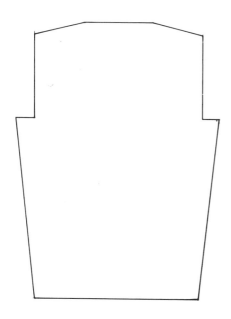

BACK: Cast on 83 (89—101) sts. Working in pattern, inc 1 st each end every ½″ 14 (18—18) times—111 (125—137) sts. Work even until piece measures 9″ (9″—9½″). Bind off 5 (6—7) sts at beg of next 2 rows. Dec 1 st each end every other row 9 (9—10) times—83 (95—103) sts. Work even until armholes measure 7½″ (8″—8½″). Bind off 5 (6—7) sts at beg of next 10 rows. Bind off remaining 33 (35—33) sts.

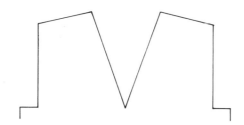

FRONT: Work same as back until armhole shaping is completed. Work to center st, attach second ball

of yarn, bind off center st, work to end of row. Dec 1 st at each neck edge every third row 16 (17—16) times. Work even until armholes measure 7½″ (8″—8½″). Bind off 5 (6—7) sts at beg of next 10 rows.

SLEEVES: Cast on 56 (59—62) sts. Inc 1 st each end every 1½″ (1¼″—1″) 11 (13—15) times—78 (85—92) sts. Work even until sleeves measure 18″ (18½″—19″). Bind off 5 (6—7) sts at beg of next 2 rows. Dec 1 st each end every other row 24 (26—28) times. Bind off remaining 20 (21—22) sts.

FINISHING: Sew shoulder, side, and sleeve seams. Set in sleeves. With right side facing, work 1 row sc around all edges.

3

NAVY LINEN VEST

LIGHTWEIGHT SWEATERS • EASY

It's the linen yarn that makes this utterly plain vest so suave.

Sizes: Men's small (medium—large).

Materials: Frederick J. Fawcett's 10/2 Linen, navy, ½ (¾—1) pound. Knitting needles, #1; circular knitting needle, #1, 29 inches long.

Gauge: 6 stitches = 1"; 9 rows = 1".

Pattern: K 1, p 1 ribbing; stockinette stitch.

A PHOTOGRAPH OF THE NAVY LINEN VEST APPEARS ON THE NEXT-TO-LAST PAGE OF THE COLOR SECTION.

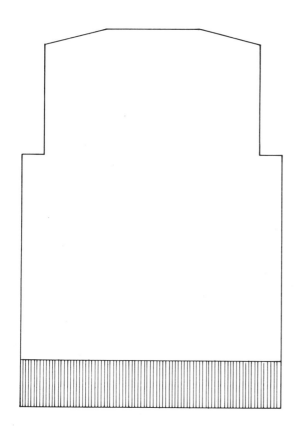

row. Working on both sides at once, bind off 4 (5—6) sts at beg of next 8 rows.

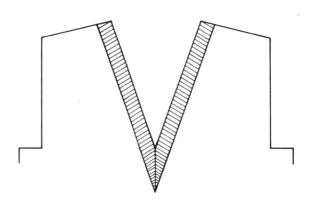

FRONT: Work same as back until piece measures 2″ less than back to underarms. Work to within 2 sts of center st, dec 1 st, attach second ball of yarn, dec 1 st, work to end of row. Dec 1 st each side of neck edge every fourth row 22 (23—23) times and at the same time, work armholes and shoulders as for back.

FINISHING: Block sweater pieces. Sew shoulder and side seams. With right side facing and circular needle, pick up and k 102 (108—114) sts around each armhole edge. Work in k 1, p 1 ribbing for 1″. Bind off in ribbing. With right side facing and circular needle, pick up and k 184 (192—198) sts around neck, including 1 st at center front. Work in k 1, p 1 ribbing for 1″, decreasing 1 st each side of center front on every row. Bind off in ribbing.

BACK: Cast on 114 (126—138) sts. Work in k 1, p 1 ribbing for 2″. Work even in stockinette st until piece measures 12″ (12½″—13″). Bind off 8 (9—10) sts at beg of next 2 rows. Dec 1 st each end every other row 10 (10—11) times—78 (88—96) sts. Work even until armholes measure 7½″ (8″—8½″). Work 16 (20—24) sts. Place center 46 (48—48) sts on holder. Attach second ball of yarn and finish

4

FLOWER SWEATER

LIGHTWEIGHT SWEATERS • EASY

This plain cotton knit is decorated with a neatly trimmed lawn, a fanciful flower, and crisp touches of white at the neckline and sleeves. The basic shape is a good one and can be elaborated with a whole flower garden or left unadorned, if you wish.

Sizes: Women's small (medium—large).

Materials: Coats and Clark's Speed-Cro-Sheen, 9 (10—11) spools aqua, 3 (4—5) spools hunter green, 2½ (3½—4½) spools white, and 2 yards yellow (any washable yarn you have on hand). Knitting needles, #7, and #5. Circular knitting needle, #7, 39 inches long. Tapestry needle for working duplicate stitch. Gauge: 5 stitches = 1″; 6 rows = 1″.

Pattern: K 1, p 1 ribbing; stockinette stitch; seed stitch.

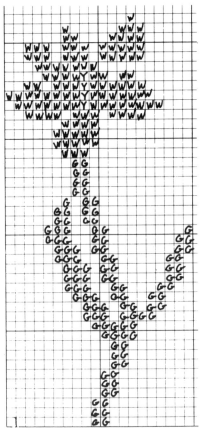

W = white
G = green
Y = yellow

A PHOTOGRAPH OF THE FLOWER SWEATER APPEARS ON PAGE 4 OF THE COLOR SECTION.

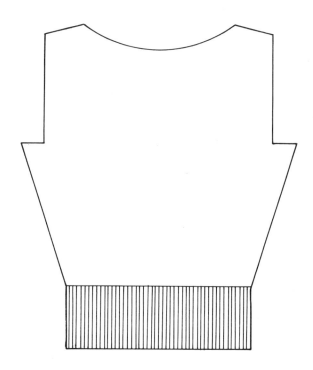

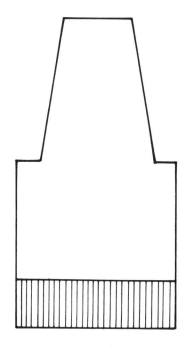

BACK: With smaller needles, using green, cast on 75 (85—95) sts. Work in k 1, p 1 ribbing for 4". Change to larger needles. Working in stockinette st, using aqua, inc 1 st each end every 1½" 5 times—85 (95—105) sts. Work even until piece measures 12". Bind off 5 sts at beg of next 2 rows. Dec 1 st each end every other row 6 (7—8) times—63 (71—79) sts. Work even until armholes measure 3" (3½"—4"). Work across first 26 (30—34) sts, place center 11 sts on holder, attach second ball of yarn and work across remaining 26 (30—34) sts. Working on both sides at once, dec 1 st at each neck edge every other row 8 (9—10) times—18 (21—24) sts on each side. Work even until armholes measure 7½" (8"—8½"). Bind off 6 (7—8) sts at each arm edge every other row 3 times.

FRONT: Work same as back.

SLEEVES: With smaller needles, using white, cast on 50 (55—60) sts. Work in k 1, p 1 ribbing for 1". Change to larger needles. Working in stockinette st, using aqua, inc 1 st each end every ¾" 5 times—60 (65—70) sts. Work even until sleeve measures 6". Bind off 5 sts at beg of next 2 rows. Dec 1 st each end every other row 18 (20—22) times. Bind off remaining 14 (15—16) sts.

FINISHING: Block pieces. Sew shoulder, side, and sleeve seams. Set in sleeves. With right side facing and using circular needle and white, pick up and k 100 sts around neck, including sts on holders. Work in seed stitch (see page 7) for 1". Bind off in seed stitch. Following diagram, work flower in duplicate st, beginning bottom of flower stem on first row after ribbing, 14 sts from side seam.

5

SHELL STITCH CROCHETED LINEN CARDIGAN

LIGHTWEIGHT SWEATERS • MEDIUM

This classic jacket will zip along with amazing speed. The linen yarn is reasonably priced, but the jacket does eat up a lot of it.

Sizes: Women's small (medium—large).

Materials: Frederick J. Fawcett's 10/5 Linen, 1 (1½—2) pound brown; ½ (1—1) pound each Spanish gold, gold, yellow; 2 (3—4) skeins each medium blue and light blue. (Note: Fawcett's linens are sold in ½- and 1-pound tubes and in 30-yard skeins. Since so little of each shade of blue is required, they should be bought in the smaller quantities.) Aluminum crochet hook, G. 1½ yards brown grosgrain ribbon to face front edges.

Gauge: One shell = 1½″ across, ¾″ high.

Pattern (multiple of 6 stitches plus 1): Row 1: 4 dc in fourth chain from hook (first shell), *skip next 2 ch, sc in next ch, skip next 2 ch, 5 dc (shell) in next ch, repeat from *, end 1 sc. Ch 3, turn. Row 2: 4 dc in first sc (first shell), *1 sc in third dc of next shell, 5 dc (shell) in next sc, repeat from *, end 1 sc. Ch 3, turn. Repeat row 2 for pattern.

Color Pattern: 2 rows brown, 1 row Spanish gold, 1 row gold, 1 row yellow. Finish neckline with 1 row medium blue, 1 row light blue. Start sleeves with 2 rows medium blue, 1 row light blue.

A PHOTOGRAPH OF THE SHELL STITCH CROCHETED LINEN CARDIGAN APPEARS ON THE NEXT-TO-LAST PAGE OF THE COLOR SECTION.

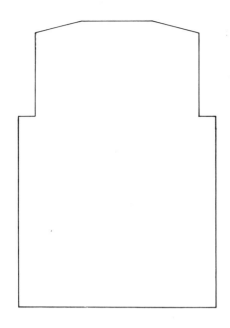

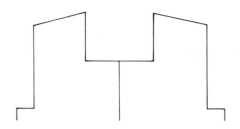

Work even until piece measures 13½" (13½"—14"), end at side edge. Skip first 1 (1½—2) shells, work across row—4½ (4½—5) shells. Work even until armhole measures 3½" (4"—4½"), end at front edge. Skip 2½ (2½—2) shells at beg of next row. Work even until armhole measures 7½" (8"—8½"), end at arm edge. Skip first 1 (1—1½) shells at beg of next row. Work to last 1 (1—1½) shells on next row. Fasten off.

RIGHT FRONT: Work same as left front.

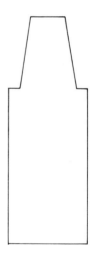

BACK: Ch 67 (76—85) sts. *For small and large sizes only*: Work rows 1 and 2 of pattern—11 (14) shells. Repeat row 2 for pattern. *For medium size only*: Row 1: 2 dc in fourth ch from hook (½ shell), work from * on row 1 of pattern to last 6 sts, skip next 2 ch, sc in next ch, skip next 2 ch, 3 dc in last ch (½ shell), ch 1, turn—12 shells. Row 2: sc in first dc, *5 dc (shell) in next sc, 1 sc in third dc of next 5 dc shell, repeat from *, end 5 dc shell in last sc, sc in top of ch-3, ch 3, turn. Row 3: 2 dc in first sc (½ shell), *sc in third dc of next shell, 5 dc in next sc, repeat from *, end sc in third dc of last shell, 3 dc in last sc, ch 1, turn. Repeat rows 2 and 3 for pattern. *For all sizes*: Work even until piece measures 13½" (13½"—14"). Break off. Turn. Skip first 1 (1½—2) shells (including ½ shells), work in pattern to last 1 (1½—2) shells—(9—10) shells. Work even in pattern until armholes measure 7½" (8"—8½"). Turn. Skip 1 (1—1½) shells at beg of next 4 rows—5 (5—4) shells. Fasten off.

LEFT FRONT: Ch 34 (40—43). *For small size only*: Row 1: Work row 1 of pattern, end 3 dc in last ch (½ shell)—5½ shells. *For medium size only*: Row 1: Work as for medium size on back—6 shells. *For large size only*: Row 1: Work row 1 of pattern —7 shells. *For all sizes*: Mark last st for front edge.

SLEEVES: Chain 49 (52—55) sts. Work same as back for 9" (9½"—10"). Fasten off. Skip first 1 (1½—2) shells, work in pattern to last 1 (1½—2) shells. Skip ½ shell each end every 2 (3—3) rows, 4 (3—3) times. Fasten off.

FINISHING: Sew shoulder, side, and sleeve seams. Set in sleeves. Work 2 rows in pattern around neck edge. Sew ribbon to wrong sides of center front edges.

6

COTTON BEACH JACKET

LIGHTWEIGHT SWEATERS • MEDIUM

White and four shades of rose were used for this lightweight cotton jacket. Wear it at the beach or on a summer evening over white pants. Nothing about it is difficult, but a beginner should become familiar with knitting techniques before attempting it.

Sizes: Women's small (medium—large).

Materials: Lily 4-strand filler, 2½ (3—3½) skeins of four shades of main and one contrasting color. Colors used for this sweater were baby pink (#47), light rose (#43), dark rose (#44), deep rose (#104), and white (#1). Knitting needles, #9.

Gauge: 4½ stitches = 1"; 4 rows = 1".

Pattern (multiple of 11 stitches plus 2): Row 1: K 1, *(k 2 tog) twice, (yo, k 1) 3 times, yo (k 2 tog) twice, repeat from *, end k 1. Row 2: P. Garter stitch at bottom of back, front, and sleeves, and along front center edges.

Color Pattern: Body of sweater: 12 rows of each shade of main color, working from darkest to lightest; 4 rows of contrasting color. Sleeves: Alternate 4 rows of each shade of main color, working from dark to light, with 12 rows of contrasting color.

PHOTOGRAPHS OF THE COTTON BEACH JACKET APPEAR ON THE FRONT COVER AND ON THE LAST PAGE OF THE COLOR SECTION.

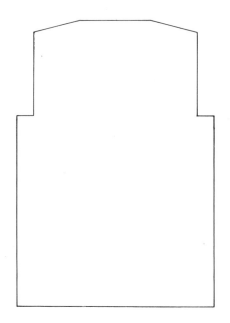

Dec 1 st at same edge every other row 5 (6—7) times—35 (40—43) sts. Work even until armhole measures 3", ending at front edge. Bind off 13 sts at beg of next row. Dec 1 st at same edge every other row 4 (6—6) times. Work even until armhole measures 7½" (8"—8½"), ending at arm edge. Bind off 6 (7—8) sts every other row 3 times.

RIGHT FRONT: Cast on 45 (51—56) sts. Work in garter st for 1". *For small and large sizes only:* **Row 1:** K 5 (front band), place marker on needle, (k 1, yo) twice, (k 2 tog) twice, repeat from * of row 1 of pattern across. *For medium size only:* **Row 1:** K 5 (front band), place marker on needle, work row 1 of pattern across. Complete to correspond to left front, reversing all shaping.

BACK: Cast on 79 (90—101) sts. Work in garter st for 1". Work even in pattern until piece measures 18" (18½"—19"). Bind off 5 (5—6) sts at beg of next 2 rows. Dec 1 st each end every other row 5 (6—7) times—59 (68—75) sts. Work even until armholes measure 7½" (8"—8½"). Bind off 6 (7—8) sts at beg of next 6 rows. Bind off remaining 23 (26—27) sts.

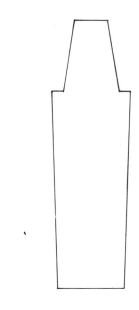

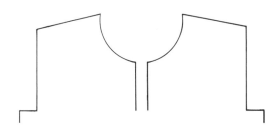

LEFT FRONT: Cast on 45 (51—56) sts. Work in garter st for 1". *For small and large sizes only:* Row 1: Work row 1 of pattern to last 11 sts, (k 2 tog) twice, (yo, k 1) twice, place marker on needle, k 5 (front band). *For medium size only:* Row 1: Work row 1 of pattern to last 5 sts, place marker on needle, k 5 (front band). Working front band sts in garter st and remaining sts in pattern, work even until piece measures 18" (18½"—19"), ending at arm edge. Bind off 5 (5—6) sts at beg of next row.

SLEEVES: Cast on 46 sts. Work in garter st for 1". Working in pattern, inc 1 st each end every 3" (2½"—2") 4 (7—9) times, working added sts in stockinette st—54 (60—64) sts. Work even until piece measures 18" (18½"—19"). Bind off 5 (5—6) sts at beg of next 2 rows. Dec 1 st each end every other row 12 (13—14) times. Bind off remaining 20 (24—24) sts.

FINISHING: Sew shoulder, side and sleeve seams. Set in sleeves. With right side facing and last color worked, work one row sc around neck.

LINEN BOAT NECK PULLOVER

LIGHTWEIGHT SWEATERS • MEDIUM

There's something about linen that makes even the plainest sweater special. It becomes more beautiful with each washing and at last purchase was a good deal cheaper than wool. Try it. If you've never worked with it before you're in for a pleasant surprise.

Sizes: Men's small (medium—large).

Materials: Frederick J. Fawcett's 10/5 Linen, 2½ (2½—3) pounds natural, 1 (1—1) pound each brown and white. Knitting needles, #8 and #6.

Gauge: 4½ stitches = 1″; 5½ rows = 1″.

Pattern: K 1, p 1 ribbing; stockinette stitch; seed stitch.

PHOTOGRAPHS OF THE LINEN BOAT NECK PULL-OVER APPEAR ON THE BACK COVER AND ON PAGE 5 OF THE COLOR SECTION.

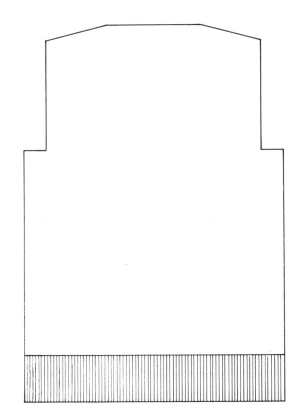

Bind off 6 (8—9) sts at beg of next 4 rows—44 (44—46) sts. Change to smaller needles. Work in k 1, p 1 ribbing for 1″. Bind off in ribbing.

FRONT: Work same as back, working brown seed st and white stockinette st stripes at center front above ribbing same as for back.

BACK: With smaller needles, cast on 86 (96—104) sts. Work k 1, p 1 ribbing for 2½″. Change to larger needles. Work even in stockinette st until piece measures 15″. At the same time, work the following color pattern, which is centered, beginning on the first row after the ribbing. The brown sections are worked in the seed stitch, the white in stockinette: 4B, 2W (70 rows high), 4B, 2W (82 rows high), 6B (94 rows high), 2W, 4B (82 rows high), 2W, 4B (70 rows high). When the back measures 15″ from beg, bind off 5 sts at beg of next 2 rows. Dec 1 st each end every other row 4 (5—6) times—68 (76—82) sts. Work even until armholes measure 8½″ (9″—9½″).

SLEEVES: With smaller needles, cast on 40 (42—44) sts. Work in k 1, p 1 ribbing for 2½″. Change to larger needles. Working in stockinette st, inc 1 st each end every 1″ 14 (15—17) times—68 (72—78) sts. Work even until piece measures 18½″ (19″—19½″). Bind off 5 sts at beg of next 2 rows. Dec 1 st each end every other row 17 (19—21) times. Bind off remaining 24 (26—26) sts.

FINISHING: Block pieces. Sew shoulder, side, and sleeve seams. Set in sleeves.

8

RASPBERRY MOHAIR PULLOVER

MEDIUM-WEIGHT SWEATERS • EASY

If you want a subtle mohair sweater (if there is such a thing), don't choose this color, which looks like cotton candy gone berserk. For all of its feather weight, mohair is surprisingly warm. It's also hard to rip out, so if you make any mistakes in the pattern, you'd probably best learn to live with them.

Sizes: Women's small (medium—large).

Materials: Reynolds' #1 Mohair, color #68, 5 (6--7) skeins. Knitting needles, #4.

Gauge: 9 stitches = 2″; 6 rows = 1″.

Pattern (multiple of 6 stitches plus 1): Rows 1, 3, 5, 7: K 1, *yo, k 2 tog, k 4, repeat from *. Row 2 and all even rows: K. Rows 9, 11, 13, 15: K 1, *k 2, yo, k 2 tog, k 2, repeat from *. Rows 17, 19, 21, 23: K 1, *k 4, yo, k 2 tog, repeat from *. Garter stitch at bottom of back, front, and sleeves, and for collar.

A PHOTOGRAPH OF THE RASPBERRY MOHAIR PULLOVER APPEARS ON PAGE 5 OF THE COLOR SECTION.

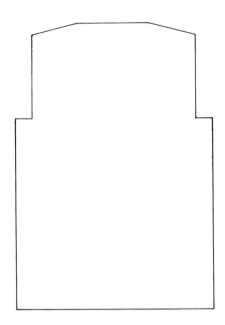

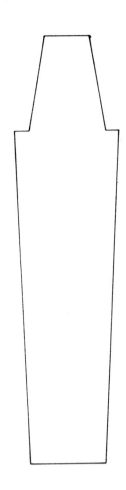

BACK: Cast on 79 (85—97) sts. Work in garter st for 2″. Work in pattern until piece measures 12″. Bind off 5 (5—6) sts at beg of next 2 rows. Dec 1 st each end every other row 5 (5—7) times—59 (65—71) sts. Work even until armholes measure 7½″ (8″—8½″). Bind off 6 (7—8) sts at beg of next 6 rows. Bind off remaining 23 sts.

SLEEVES: Cast on 37 sts. Work in garter st for 2″. Working in pattern, inc 1 st each end every 1½″ (1¼″—1¼″) 9 (11—13) times—55 (59—63) sts. Work even until piece measures 18″ (18½″—19″). Bind off 5 (5—6) sts at beg of next 2 rows. Dec 1 st each end every other row 10 (12—14) times. Bind off remaining 25 (25—23) sts.

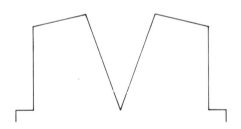

FRONT: Work same as back until armholes measure 2″ (2½″--3″)—59 (65—71) sts. Work across to center st, attach second ball of yarn, bind off center st, work across row—29 (32—35) sts on each side. Working on both sides at once, dec 1 st at each neck edge every other row 11 times—18 (21—24) sts on each side. Work even until armholes measure 7½″ (8″—8½″). Bind off 6 (7—8) sts at beg of next 6 rows.

COLLAR: Cast on 41 sts. Working in garter st, inc 1 st each end every other row until piece measures 2½″. Bind off.

FINISHING: Sew shoulder, side, and sleeve seams. Set in sleeves. Sew collar in place.

9

SWEATER WITH COWBOY

MEDIUM-WEIGHT SWEATERS • MEDIUM

Take a classic crew neck and embellish it with a motif of your choice. Here we used the duplicate stitch to create a colorful cowboy once this simple sweater was finished. If you wish, you could work the cowboy in as you go, using the Fair Isle method (see Windmill Sweater, page 42). Try them both and see which technique you like better. Follow the chart and you can have your own cowboy. Or follow the instructions on page 14 for making pictures, and you can have anything you want on your sweater.

Sizes: Men's small (medium—large).

Materials: Bucilla's Knitting Worsted, 5 (6—7) skeins yellow for body of sweater. Several yards of brown, black, blue, red for cowboy and horse. If you don't have scraps of these colors in knitting worsted, either borrow from friends or buy some Persian yarn, which can be purchased in small quantities. Paternayan is our recommendation. Knitting needles, #8 and #6. Yarn needle for duplicate stitch.

Gauge: 4 stitches = 1″; 5½ rows = 1″.

Pattern: K 1, p 1 ribbing; stockinette stitch.

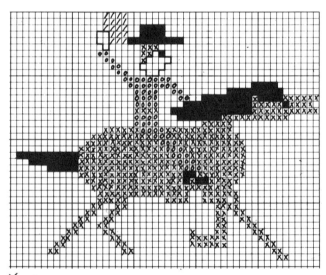

X = brown
■ = black
O = blue
□ = white
/ = red

A PHOTOGRAPH OF THE SWEATER WITH COWBOY APPEARS ON PAGE 5 OF THE COLOR SECTION.

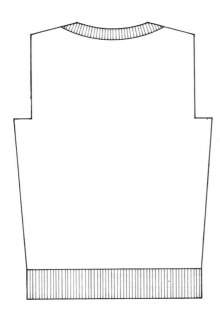

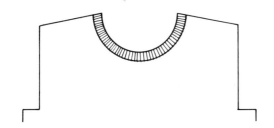

BACK: With smaller needles, cast on 76 (84—92) sts. Work in k 1, p 1 ribbing for 2″. Change to larger needles and work even in stockinette st until piece measures 15″. Bind off 4 sts at beg of next 2 rows. Dec 1 st each end every other row 4 (5—6) times— 60 (66—72) sts. Work even until armholes measure 8½″ (9″—9½″). Bind off 6 (7—8) sts at beg of next 6 rows. Bind off remaining 24 sts.

FRONT: Work same as back until armholes measure 5½″ (6″—6½″). Work across first 25 (28—31) sts. Attach second ball of yarn and bind off center 10 sts, work across remaining 25 (28—31) sts. Working

on both sides at once, dec 1 st at each neck edge every other row 7 times—18 (21—24) sts on each side. Work even until armholes measure 8½″ (9″—9½″). Bind off 6 (7—8) sts at each arm edge every other row 3 times.

SLEEVES: With smaller needles, cast on 36 (36—38) sts. Work in k 1, p 1 ribbing for 2″. Change to larger needles. Working in stockinette st, inc 1 st each end every 1″ 12 (14—15) times—60 (64—68) sts. Work even until sleeves measure 18½″ (19″—19½″). Bind off 4 sts at beg of next 2 rows. Dec 1 st each end every other row 15 (17—19) times. Bind off remaining 22 sts.

FINISHING: Block. Sew left shoulder seam. Using smaller needles, pick up and k 88 sts around neck edge. Work in k 1, p 1 ribbing for 1″. Bind off in ribbing. Sew right shoulder, side, and sleeve seams. Set in sleeves. Following diagram, work cowboy in duplicate st. Cowboy measures 49 sts across, 38 sts up and down. Center on front of sweater, placing highest point 3 inches below neckline ribbing.

10

RED, WHITE, AND BROWN TWEED CARDIGAN

MEDIUM-WEIGHT SWEATERS • MEDIUM

I love the way these three colors look together, but any three contrasting colors will work well in this simple slip stitch pattern, with each color worked for two rows. People will look at it and marvel at the talent in your nimble fingers.

Sizes: Women's small (medium—large).

Materials: Bucilla's Wool and Shetland Wool, 3 (4—5) skeins each java (240), fireball (345), and white (1). Knitting needles, #8. Aluminum crochet hook, size E. 2 yards ½″ grosgrain ribbon. 6 ¾″ buttons.

Gauge: 7 stitches = 1″; 5½ rows = 1″.

Pattern (multiple of 2 stitches plus 2): Work 2 rows in each color, alternating the three colors. **Row 1:** K 1, *sl 1 with yarn in back, k 1, repeat from *, end k 1. **Row 2:** K 1, *p 1, sl 1 with yarn in front, repeat from *, end k 1. **Row 3:** K 1, *k 1, sl 1 with yarn in back, repeat from *, end k 1. **Row 4:** K 1, *sl 1 with yarn in front, p 1, repeat from *, end sl 1, p 1, k 1.

A PHOTOGRAPH OF THE RED, WHITE, AND BROWN TWEED CARDIGAN APPEARS ON PAGE 2 OF THE COLOR SECTION.

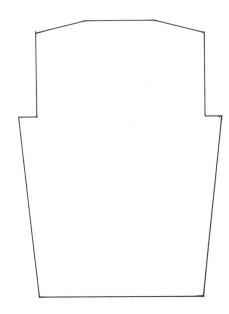

BACK: Cast on 106 (114—120) sts. Working in pattern, inc 1 st each end every 1½" (1¾"—1¾") 7 (10—14) times—120 (134—148) sts. Work even until piece measures 13½". Bind off 8 sts at beg of next 2 rows. Dec 1 st each end every other row 8 (10—11) times—88 (98—110) sts. Work even until armholes measure 7½" (8"—8½"). Bind off 8 (9—11) sts at beg of next 6 rows. Bind off remaining 40 (44—44) sts.

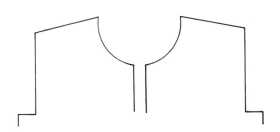

LEFT FRONT: Cast on 60 (64—66) sts. Working in pattern, inc 1 st at side edge every 1½" (1¾"—1¾") 7 (10—14) times—67 (74—80) sts. Work even until piece measures 13½", ending at side edge. Bind off 8 sts at beg of next row. Dec 1 st at arm edge every other row 8 (10—11) times—51 (56—61) sts. Work even until armhole measures 4½" (5"—5½"), ending at front edge. Bind off 18 sts at beg of next row. Dec 1 st at neck edge every row 9 (11—10) times—24 (27—33) sts. Work even until armhole measures 7½" (8"—8½"). At arm edge

bind off 8 (9—11) sts every other row 3 times. Place 6 stitch markers evenly spaced along center edge for buttons.

RIGHT FRONT: Work as for left front, reversing shaping and making 6 buttonholes opposite markers as follows: Beg at front edge, work 2 sts, bind off next 4 sts, work across row. On the following row, cast on 4 sts over those bound off.

SLEEVES: Cast on 58 (60—62) sts. Working in pattern, inc 1 st every 1" 13 (16—18) times—84 (92—98) sts. Work even until piece measures 18" (18½"—19"). Bind off 8 sts at beg of next 2 rows. Dec 1 st each end every other row 18 (20—22) times. Bind off remaining 32 (36—38) sts.

COLLAR: Cast on 90 (94—98) sts. Working in pattern, inc 1 st each end every other row until piece measures 3". Bind off.

FINISHING: Sew shoulder, side, and sleeve seams. Set in sleeves. Sew collar in place. With right side facing, work 1 row sc around all edges. Sew ribbon to inside of front edges, making slits for buttonholes. Sew on buttons.

11

MULTI-COLORED PASTEL CARDIGAN WITH RIDGES

MEDIUM-WEIGHT SWEATERS • MEDIUM

The pastel colors give this version of the sweater its ice-cream cone look. It could also be done in one solid color with contrasting or complementary ridges, or in a solid color with ridges in all different colors (if you want to use up lots of small scraps of yarn). Place the ridges closer together; move them farther apart. Make it your *sweater.*

PHOTOGRAPHS OF THE MULTICOLORED PASTEL CARDIGAN WITH RIDGES APPEAR ON THE FRONT COVER AND ON THE LAST PAGE OF THE COLOR SECTION.

Sizes: Women's small (medium—large).

Materials: Spinnerin's Marvel-Twist Deluxe Knitting Worsted, 1 (1½—2) skein each of baby pink (401), baby blue (402), yellow (they call it vanilla—404), crystal green (403), and ½ (¾—1) skein white (400). Knitting needles, #8 and #6. 1½ yards grosgrain ribbon. 6 ¾″ buttons.

Gauge: 4 stitches = 1″; 5½ rows = 1″.

Pattern: K 1, p 1 ribbing; stockinette stitch; white ridge is made by knitting two rows of white.

Color Pattern: Ribbing, 2 rows each of pink, blue, yellow, green. Body, 6 rows pink, white ridge, 1 row blue, 1 row yellow, 1 row green, 1 row pink, white ridge, 6 rows blue, white ridge, 1 row yellow, 1 row green, 1 row pink, 1 row blue, white ridge, 6 rows yellow, white ridge, 1 row green, 1 row pink, 1 row blue, 1 row yellow, white ridge, 6 rows green, white ridge, 1 row pink, 1 row blue, 1 row yellow, 1 row green, white ridge, Repeat from beginning of body.

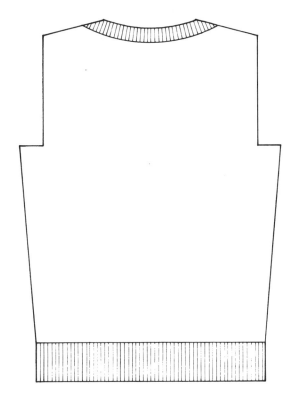

BACK: Using smaller needles, cast on 52 (56—60) sts. Work in k 1, p 1 ribbing in color pattern for 2½". Change to larger needles. Working in color pattern and stockinette st with ridges, inc 1 st each end every ¾" 8 (10—12) times—68 (76—84) sts. Work even until piece measures 12". Bind off 6 sts at beg of next 2 rows. Dec 1 st each end every other row 3 (4—5) times—50 (56—62) sts. Work even until armholes measure 7½" (8"—8½"). Bind off 5 (6—7) sts at beg of next 6 rows. Place remaining 20 sts on holder.

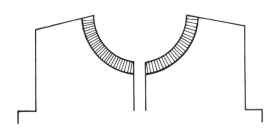

LEFT FRONT: Using smaller needles, cast on 30 (32—34) sts. Work in k 1, p 1 ribbing in color pattern for 2½". Change to larger needles. Working in color pattern and stockinette st with ridges, inc 1 st at side edge every ¾" 8 (10—12) times—38 (42—46) sts. Work even until piece measures 12", ending at side edge. Bind off 6 sts at beg of next row. Dec 1 st at arm edge every other row 3 (4—5) times—29 (32—35) sts. Work even until armhole measures 4½" (5"—

5½"), ending at front edge. Place first 8 sts on holder. Dec 1 st at neck edge every row 6 times, then work even until armhole measures 7½" (8"—8½"). At arm edge bind off 5 (6—7) sts every other row 3 times. Place 6 stitch markers evenly spaced along center edge for buttons.

RIGHT FRONT: Work to correspond to left front, reversing shaping and making 6 buttonholes opposite markers as follows: Beg at front edge, work 2 sts, bind off next 2 sts, work across row. On the following row, cast on 2 sts over those bound off.

SLEEVES: Using smaller needles, cast on 32 (34—36) sts. Work k 1, p 1 ribbing in color pattern for 2½". Change to larger needles. Working in color pattern and stockinette st, inc 1 st each end every 1" 8 (9—10) times—48 (52—56) sts. Work even until piece measures 18" (18½"—19"). Bind off 6 sts at beg of next 2 rows. Dec 1 st each end every other row 15 (16—17) times. Bind off remaining 6 (8—10) sts.

FINISHING: Sew shoulder, side, and sleeve seams. Set in sleeves. With right side facing and smaller needles, pick up and k 60 sts around neck, including sts on holders. Work in k 1, p 1 ribbing for 1". Bind off in ribbing. With right side facing, and any color you wish, work 1 row sc along front edges. Sew ribbon to wrong sides of front edges, making slits for buttonholes. Sew on buttons.

12

THREE GRAYS AND RED SWEATER

MEDIUM-WEIGHT SWEATERS • MEDIUM

Like all the best sweater patterns, this one creates a marvelously complex sweater with the simplest stitches and techniques. The vertical red lines are worked right along with the sweater in the slip stitch, and the gray squares achieve their marvelous texture with the seed stitch. The only thing you have to be careful of is to carry the red yarn loosely across the back so the sweater doesn't pull together. Hold two fingers between the yarn and the work as you slip stitches to keep the yarn loose.

Sizes: Women's small (medium—large).

Materials: Reynolds' Classique, 4 (4½—5) skeins each of three shades of gray: light (2507, color D), medium (2508, color C), dark (2535, color B), and 2 (2¼—2½) skeins of red (2540, color A). Knitting needles, #6.

Gauge: 5½ stitches = 1″; 6 rows = 1″.

Pattern (multiple of 6 stitches plus 5): Cast on with [color] A [red]. Row 1: With [color] B, [dark gray] *k 5, sl 1 with yarn in back, repeat from *, end k 5. Row 2: With B, *k 1, p 1, k 1, p 1, k 1, sl 1 with yarn in front, repeat from *, end p 1, k 1. Rows 3 and 4: Repeat row 2, slipping with yarn in back for row 3, with yarn in front for row 4. Row 5: With A, k 1, sl 4 with yarn in back, *k 1, sl 5 with yarn in back, repeat from *, end k 1. Row 6: With A, p 1, sl 4 with yarn in front, *p 1, sl 5 with yarn in front, repeat from *, end p 1. Rows 7-10: Repeat row 2, slipping with yarn in back on odd rows, with yarn in front on even rows. Row 11: With A, k. Row 12: With A, p. Rows 13-24: Repeat rows 1-12, replacing color B with color C and leaving color A where specified. Rows 25-36: Repeat rows 1-12, replacing color C with color D and leaving color A where specified. *Note*: Always slip with yarn in back on odd rows, slip with yarn in front on even rows.

A PHOTOGRAPH OF THE THREE GRAYS AND RED SWEATER APPEARS ON PAGE 5 OF THE COLOR SECTION.

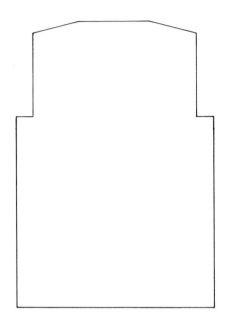

BACK: Cast on 95 (107—119) sts. Work even in pattern until piece measures 16″ (16″—16½″). Bind off 7 sts at beg of next 2 rows. Dec 1 st each end every other row 6 (8—9) times—69 (77—87) sts. Work even until armholes measure 7½″ (8″—8½″). Bind off 5 (6—7) sts at beg of next 8 rows. Bind off remaining 29 (29—31) sts.

SLEEVES: Cast on 47 sts. Working in pattern, inc 1 st each end every ½″ 10 (13—15) times—67 (73—77) sts. Work even until piece measures 18″ (18½″—19″). Bind off 7 sts at beg of next 2 rows. Dec 1 st each end every other row 18 (20—22) times. Bind off remaining 17 (19—19) sts.

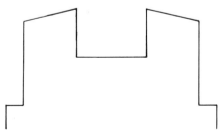

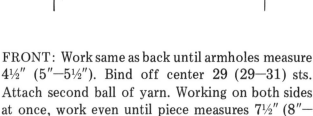

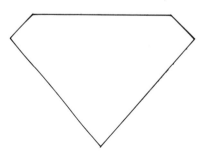

FRONT: Work same as back until armholes measure 4½″ (5″—5½″). Bind off center 29 (29—31) sts. Attach second ball of yarn. Working on both sides at once, work even until piece measures 7½″ (8″—8½″). Bind off 5 (6—7) sts at beg of next 8 rows.

COLLAR: Cast on 59 sts. Working in pattern, inc 1 st each end and each side of center red st every other row until piece is 3″ wide at points. Bind off.

FINISHING: Sew shoulder, side, and sleeve seams. Set in sleeves. Sew collar in place.

13

WINDMILL SWEATER

MEDIUM-WEIGHT SWEATERS • ADVANCED

Three windmills sit solidly under the truncated V-neck of this three-color pull-over. Colors here are not slip stitched, but are worked Fair Isle style, changing as necessary across the row. Just follow the color pattern, remembering to twist the strands around each other when you change colors so there won't be any holes. The same color will be carried in a couple of places in the same row. The easiest way to do this is to secure a length of each color around a small piece of slit cardboard that will act as a spool. This is much neater than working each color from its own big skein.

Sizes: Men's small (medium—large).

Materials: Bucilla's Knitting Worsted, 2 (2½—3) skeins each dark oxford (70), camel (368), and russet brown (384) for man's medium size. Knitting needles, #8, #6, and 4 d-p #6.

Gauge: 5 stitches = 1"; 5 rows = 1".

Pattern: K 1, p 1 ribbing; stockinette stitch.

Color Pattern: Follow graphs. Back, work squares with contrasting Xs as follows: One brown square with gray Xs, one camel square with brown Xs, one gray square with camel Xs. For the second row of squares, start with camel square with brown Xs, then gray square with camel Xs, then brown square with gray Xs. For the third row, start with gray square with camel Xs, then brown square with gray Xs, then camel square with brown Xs. Center these if the boxes don't work out evenly. However, there is nothing wrong if there is a fraction of a box at one end. Just remember to begin your next row where you left off.

A PHOTOGRAPH OF THE WINDMILL SWEATER APPEARS ON PAGE 5 OF THE COLOR SECTION.

X = brown
/ = gray
O = camel

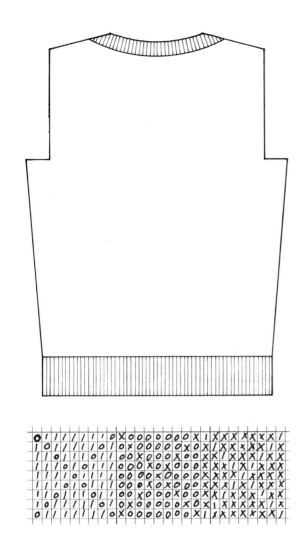

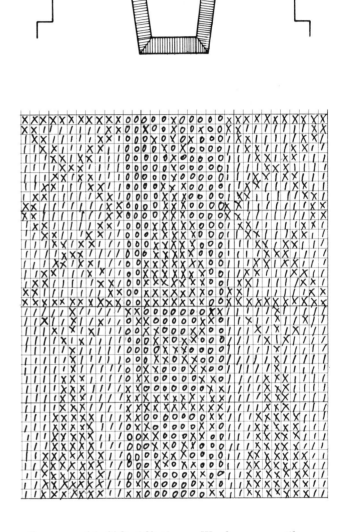

BACK: With smaller needles and camel yarn, cast on 95 (105—115) sts. Work in k 1, p 1 ribbing for 2½″. Change to larger needles. Working in stockinette st and following color pattern, work even until piece measures 15″. Bind off 5 sts at beg of next 2 rows. Dec 1 st each end every other row 5 (6—7) times—75 (83—91) sts. Work even until armholes measure 8½″ (9″—9½″). Bind off 7 (8—9) sts at beg of next 6 rows. Bind off remaining 33 (35—37) sts.

FRONT: Work same as back until 45 rows below armhole. Work the center panel (see chart above, right) across the center 33 stitches. This leaves 31 (36—41) stitches on either side, which should be continued in same pattern as back. Continue working same as back until 5 rows below armhole—75 (83—91) sts. Work across first 32 (36—40) sts, attach second ball of yarn and bind off center 11 sts, work across remaining 32 (36—40) sts. Working on both sides at once, dec 1 st at each neck edge every

other row 11 (12—13) times. Work even until armholes measure 8½″ (9″—9½″). Bind off 7 (8—9) sts at each arm edge every other row 3 times.

FINISHING: Block pieces. Sew shoulder and side seams. With d-p needles and camel, pick up and k 104 (106—108) sts around neck edge. Work k 1, p 1 ribbing for 1″. Bind off in ribbing. With d-p needles and camel, around each armhole edge pick up and k 94 (100—106) sts. Work in k 1, p 1 ribbing for 1″. Bind off in ribbing.

14

FIVE-COLOR SWEATER WITH CROCHETED BODY AND KNIT SLEEVES

MEDIUM-WEIGHT SWEATERS • ADVANCED

This is a special sweater for a number of reasons: it combines knitting and crocheting, the crocheting is done vertically instead of horizontally, and the yarn is a very pleasant soft, fat cotton. The crocheting on this whizzes along, as crocheting tends to do. For some reason, the different gauges for the different crochet stitches used here don't create any problem. Follow the diagram, starting at the lower left-hand corner and working up and down in colors and stitches shown. The sleeves are another slip stitch knitting pattern, which means that, although the colors look complicated, they're all worked two rows at a time— no need to change colors in the middle of a row.

A PHOTOGRAPH OF THE FIVE-COLOR SWEATER WITH CROCHETED BODY AND KNIT SLEEVES APPEARS ON PAGE 3 OF THE COLOR SECTION.

Sizes: Women's small (medium—large).

Materials: Lily Mills' Rug Weave Cotton (Art. 814), 3 (3½—4) skeins each brown (120, color A), rust (129, color B), dark brown (124, color C), salmon rose (41, color D), orange (20, color E). Knitting needles, #9. Aluminum crochet hook, size J.

Gauge: Body—slip stitch, 3½ stitches = 1", 5 rows = 1"; single crochet, 3 stitches = 1", 3 rows = 1"; double crochet, 2½ stitches = 1", 1 row = 1". Sleeves—4 stitches = 1", 4 rows = 1".

Pattern: For body, dc, sc, sl st as indicated on diagram. Sleeve pattern (multiple of 6 stitches plus 2): Cast on with color A and p 1 row. Row 1 (right side): With B, k 1, *sl 2 with yarn in back, k 4, repeat from *, end k 1. Row 2: With B, k 1, *k 2, p 2, sl 2 with yarn in front, repeat from *, end k 1. Row 3: With C, k 3, *sl 2 with yarn in back, k 4, repeat from *, end sl 2, k 3. Row 4: With C, k 1, *p 2, sl 2 with yarn in front, k 2, repeat from *, end k 1. Row 5: With D, k 1, *k 4, sl 2 with yarn in back, repeat from *, end k 1. Row 6: With D, k 1, *sl 2 with yarn in front, k 2, p 2, repeat from *, end k 1. Rows 7 and 8: With A, repeat rows 1 and 2. Rows 9 and 10: With B, repeat rows 3 and 4. Rows 11 and 12: With C, repeat rows 5 and 6. Rows 13 and 14: With D, repeat rows 1 and 2. Rows 15 and 16: With A, repeat rows 3 and 4. Rows 17 and 18: With B, repeat rows 5 and 6. Rows 19 and 20: With C, repeat rows 1 and 2. Rows 21 and 22: With D, repeat rows 3 and 4. Rows 23 and 24: With A, repeat rows 5 and 6.

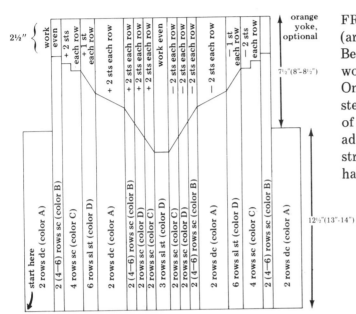

2½″ { work even

+ 2 sts each row

+ 1 st each row

— 1 st each row

— 2 sts each row

work even

+ 2 sts each row

+ 2 sts each row

+ 2 sts each row

— 2 sts each row

— 2 sts each row

— 2 sts each row

orange yoke, optional

7½″(8″-8½″)

12½″(13″-14″)

start here

2 rows dc (color A)

2 (4—6) rows sc (color B)

4 rows sc (color C)

6 rows sl st (color D)

2 rows dc (color A)

2 (4—6) rows sc (color B)

2 rows sc (color C)

2 rows sc (color C)

3 rows sl st (color D)

2 rows sc (color C)

2 rows sc (color C)

2 (4—6) rows sc (color B)

2 rows dc (color A)

6 rows sl st (color D)

4 rows sc (color C)

2 (4—6) rows sc (color B)

2 rows dc (color A)

FRONT: Begin at waist where shown on diagram (arrow) and work vertically, following the diagram. Begin the yoke 2½″ from the shoulder seam and work even until the sc rows of color D are reached. Omit the top 9 sts of the first D row for the first step down. Omit 2 additional sts in the first sc row of color C for the second step down, and skip 2 additional sts in the first sl st row of color D (center stripe) for the third. Reverse shaping for second half of front.

BACK: Begin at waist where shown on diagram (arrow) and work vertically, following the diagram. Begin yoke as indicated, 2½″ from the shoulder seam, and increase or decrease the length of the yoke section as indicated for each row.

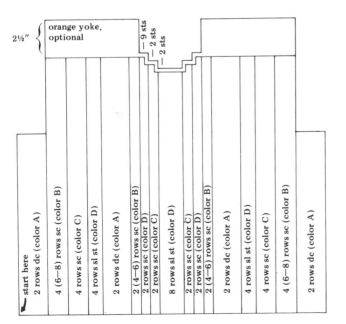

2½″ { orange yoke, optional

— 9 sts

— 2 sts

— 2 sts

start here

2 rows dc (color A)

4 (6—8) rows sc (color B)

4 rows sc (color C)

4 rows sl st (color D)

2 rows dc (color A)

2 (4—6) rows sc (color B)

2 rows sc (color C)

2 rows sc (color C)

8 rows sl st (color D)

2 rows sc (color C)

2 rows sc (color C)

2 (4—6) rows sc (color B)

2 rows dc (color A)

4 rows sl st (color D)

4 rows sc (color C)

4 (6—8) rows sc (color B)

2 rows dc (color A)

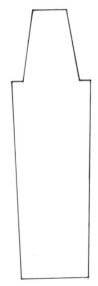

SLEEVES: Cast on 38 sts in color A. Working in pattern, inc 1 st each end every 3″ (2½″—2″) 4 (7—9) times—46 (52—56) sts. Work even until piece measures 18″ (18½″—19″). Bind off 5 (5—6) sts at beginning of next 2 rows. Dec 1 st each end every other row 12 (13—14) times. Bind off remaining 12 (16—18) sts.

FINISHING: Sew shoulder, side and sleeve seams. Set in sleeves.

15

OLIVE AND RUST SHAWL COLLAR CARDIGAN

MEDIUM-WEIGHT SWEATERS • MEDIUM

The serpentine pattern on the body of this sweater and the nubbly one on the collar are both handily done with—you guessed it—slip stitches.

PHOTOGRAPHS OF THE OLIVE AND RUST SHAWL COLLAR CARDIGAN APPEAR ON THE BACK COVER AND ON PAGE 4 OF THE COLOR SECTION.

Sizes: Men's small (medium—large).

Materials: Bucilla's Knitting Worsted, 2 (2½—3) skeins each wood brown (355, color A) and olive (360, color B). Knitting needles, #8 and #6. 4 ½" buttons.

Gauge: Body stitch, 5½ stitches = 1"; 5 rows = 1". Collar stitch, 6 stitches = 1"; 6 rows = 1".

Pattern (multiple of 6 stitches): Body and Sleeves,
Row 1: With A, k 4, sl 2 with yarn in back.
Row 2: With A, sl 2 with yarn in front, p 4.
Row 3: With B, sl 4 with yarn in back, k 2.
Row 4: With B, p 2, sl 4 with yarn in front.
Row 5: With A, repeat row 1.
Row 6: With A, repeat row 2.
Row 7: With B, k 2, sl 2 with yarn in back, k 4, end k 2.
Row 8: With B, p 2, sl 2 with yarn in front, p 4, end p 2.
Row 9: With A, sl 2 with yarn in back, k 2, sl 4 with yarn in back, end sl 2.
Row 10: With A, sl 2 with yarn in front, p 2, sl 4 with yarn in front, end sl 2.
Row 11: With B, repeat row 7.
Row 12: With B, repeat row 8.
Row 13: With A, sl 2 with yarn in back, k 4.
Row 14: With A, p 4, sl 2 with yarn in front.
Row 15: With B, k 2, sl 4 with yarn in back.
Row 16: With B, sl 4 with yarn in front, p 2.
Row 17: With A, repeat row 13.
Row 18: With A, repeat row 14.

Collar, Row 1: With A, k 1, sl 1 with yarn in back.
Row 2: With A, k 1, *k 1, sl 1 with yarn in front*, end k 1.
Row 3: With B, k 1, *k 1, sl 1 with yarn in back*, end k 1.
Row 4: With B, k 1, *sl 1 with yarn in front, k 1*, end k 1.
Garter stitch around all edges.

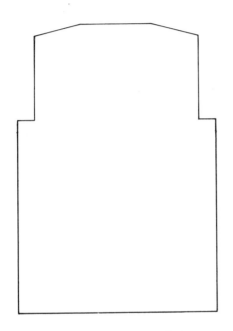

BACK: With smaller needles and A, cast on 102 (114—126) sts. Work even in garter st for 1". Change to larger needles. Working in pattern, work even until piece measures 17". Bind off 5 sts at beg of next 2 rows. Dec 1 st each end every other row 5 (6—9) times—82 (92—98) sts. Work even until armholes measure 8½" (9"—9½"). Bind off 8 (10—11) sts at beg of next 6 rows. Bind off remaining 34 (32—32) sts.

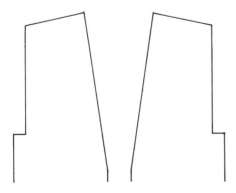

RIGHT FRONT: Using smaller needles and A, cast on 64 (69—75) sts. Work even in garter st for 1",

ending at front edge. Sl first 12 sts onto holder (front band sts). Change to larger needles. Work even in pattern on 52 (57—63) sts until piece measures 14" (14½"—15"), ending at front edge. Dec 1 st at neck edge every fourth row 16 times, and at the same time, when piece measures 18", at arm edge bind off 5 sts once, dec 1 st every other row 6 (6—9) times, then work even until armhole measures 8½" (9"—9½"), ending at arm edge. Bind off 8 (10—11) sts every other row 3 times.

LEFT FRONT: Work to correspond to right front, reversing all shaping.

SLEEVES: With smaller needles and A, cast on 48 sts. Work in garter st for 1". Change to larger needles. Working in pattern, inc 1 st each end every ¾" 17 (20—23) times—82 (88—94) sts. Work even until piece measures 18½" (19"—19½"). Bind off 5 sts at beg of next 2 rows. Dec 1 st each end every other row 20 (22—24) times. Bind off remaining 32 (34—36) sts.

RIGHT FRONT BAND AND SHAWL COLLAR:
With right side facing and using smaller needles, sl
12 sts from holder onto left-hand needle, work even
in pattern until piece measures 14″ (14½″—15″)
from lower edge. Inc 1 st at outer edge every other
row 15 times—27 sts, then work even until piece fits
around neck to center back. Bind off. Mark front
band for placement of 4 buttons evenly spaced, the
first 4″ from lower edge, the last at beg of collar
shaping.

LEFT FRONT BAND AND SHAWL COLLAR:
Work to correspond to right front band and shawl
collar, reversing all shaping and working 4 buttonholes opposite markers as follows: Starting at outer
edge, work across first 5 sts, bind off 3 sts, work
across remaining 4 sts. On the next row, cast on 3
sts over those bound off.

FINISHING: Block pieces. Sew shoulder, side, and
sleeve seams. Set in sleeves. Sew center back seam
on collar. Sew collar in place. Sew on buttons.

16

HEAVY RED JACKET

WINTER SWEATERS • EASY

A massive tree grows on the back of this jacket, one that is appropriate to the thickness of the yarn. The white mohair clouds and yellow cotton sun were added afterward. This is another sweater that can be turned out in an astonishingly short time and will provide intense winter warmth.

A PHOTOGRAPH OF THE HEAVY RED JACKET APPEARS ON PAGE 2 OF THE COLOR SECTION.

Sizes: Women's small (medium—large).

Materials: Golden Fleece's MH, medium gauge, 4 (4½—5) skeins red (102), 1 (1¼—1½) skeins brown (204), 1 (1—1) skein green (108); Reynolds #1 Mohair, 1 skein white; Coats & Clark's Knit Cro-Sheen, several yards of yellow. Knitting needles, #15. Aluminum crochet hook, size 10½. 2 yards grosgrain ribbon. 5 1½" buttons.

Gauge: 1½ stitches = 1"; 2½ rows = 1".

Pattern: Stockinette stitch, garter stitch.

Color Pattern: Follow graph. Center on back.

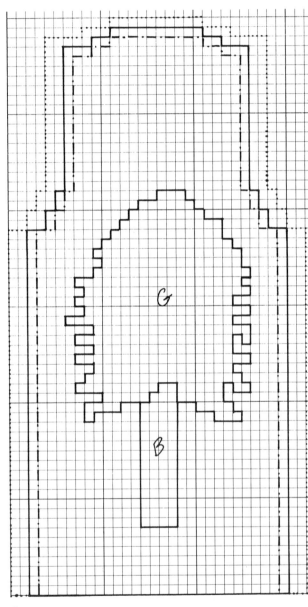

G = green
B = brown

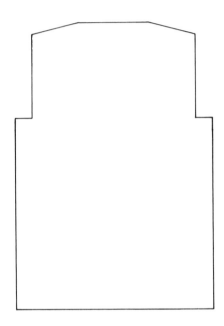

twice—18 (20—24) sts. Work even until armholes measure 7½″ (8″—8½″). Bind off 2 (3—4) sts at beg of next 2 rows, 2 (2—3) sts at beg of next 2 rows. Bind off remaining 10 sts.

RIGHT FRONT: Cast on 13 (14—16) sts. Work in stockinette st until piece measures 15″, ending at side edge. Bind off 2 sts at beg of next row, then at same edge dec 1 st every other row twice—9 (10—12) sts. Work even until armhole measures 7½″ (8″—8½″), ending at arm edge. Bind off 2 (3—4) sts at beg of next row. Work 1 row even. Bind off remaining 2 (2—3) sts. Place 5 markers evenly spaced along center edge for buttons.

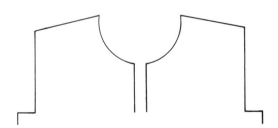

BACK: Cast on 26 (28—32) sts. Working in stockinette st and following chart for color pattern, work even until piece measures 15″. Bind off 2 sts at beg of next 2 rows. Dec 1 st each end every other row

LEFT FRONT: Work to correspond to right front, reversing all shaping, and make 5 buttonholes along center edge opposite markers as follows: Starting at front edge work first stitch, bind off 2 sts, work to end of row. On the next row, cast on 2 sts over those bound off.

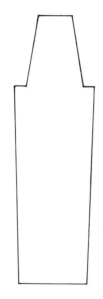

SLEEVES: Cast on 12 (13—14) sts. Working in stockinette st, inc 1 st every 4" 3 (3—4) times—18 (19—22) sts. Work even until piece measures 18" (18½"—19"). Bind off 2 sts at beg of next 2 rows. Dec 1 st each end every third row 4 (5—6) times. Bind off remaining 6 (5—6) sts.

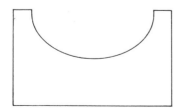

COLLAR: Cast on 28 (28—30) sts. Working in garter stitch, work even for 5". Bind off center 10 sts. Work to end of row. Decrease 1 st at center edge

every other row 4 (4—5) times. Work even for 2". Bind off. Repeat on other side of center edge.

FINISHING: With white mohair, embroider cloud shapes to the back of the jacket, as many as you wish. For sun: With yellow cotton, ch 3, join in ring with sl st. Round 1: Sc 6 into ring. Round 2: Sc 2 into each sc. Round 3: (Sc 1 into sc, sc 2 into next sc) 6 times. Round 4: (Sc into 2 sc, sc 2 into next sc) 6 times. Round 5: (Sc into 3 sc, sc 2 into next sc) 6 times. Round 6: (Sc into 4 sc, sc 2 into next sc) 6 times. Round 7: (Sc into 5 sc, sc 2 into next sc) 6 times. (42 sts.) End off. Sew sun to desired position in back of jacket. Sew shoulder, side, and sleeve seams. Set in sleeves. Sew collar to neck edge. With right side facing, work 1 row sl st around all edges.

17

HEFTY BLACK CARDIGAN WITH HOOD

WINTER SWEATERS • EASY

This is a man's sweater in concept, although a strong woman could bear its weight as well. Of course, the pattern can be figured for any weight yarn, but if there are any men out there who have toyed with the idea of taking up knitting and have hesitated because it seemed too delicate a pursuit, this is a good sweater to start on. In no way can it be considered delicate. But it is warm, and it does work up fast.

Sizes: Men's small (medium—large).

Materials: Mexiskeins medium weight yarn, 3½ (3¾—4) pounds black (70). Knitting needles, #15. Aluminum crochet hook, size 10½. 2 yards grosgrain ribbon. 5 1¾" buttons.

Gauge: 1½ stitches = 1"; 2 rows = 1".

Pattern: Stockinette stitch.

A PHOTOGRAPH OF THE HEFTY BLACK CARDIGAN WITH HOOD APPEARS ON PAGE 3 OF THE COLOR SECTION.

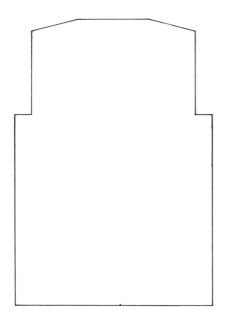

BACK: Cast on 28 (32—36) sts. Work even in stocki-nette st for 15½″ (16″—16″). Bind off 2 sts at beg of next 2 rows. Work even 1 row. Dec 1 st each end of next row—22 (26—28) sts. Work even until armholes measure 8½″ (9″—9½″). Bind off 3 (4—5) sts at beg of next 4 rows. Bind off remaining 10 sts.

SLEEVES: Cast on 13 (14—14) sts. Working in stockinette st, inc 1 st each end every 3″ (3″—2½″) 5 (5—6) times—23 (24—26) sts. Work even until piece measures 18½″ (19″—19½″). Bind off 3 (4—5) sts at beg of next 2 rows. Dec 1 st each end every other row 5 (6—6) times. Bind off remaining 7 (4—4) sts.

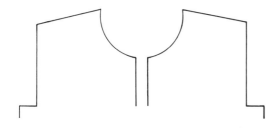

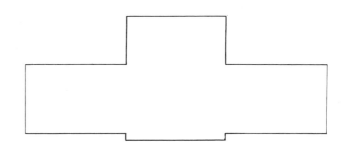

RIGHT FRONT: Cast on 16 (18—19) sts. Work even in stockinette st for 15½″ (16″—16″), end at side edge. Bind off 2 sts at beg of next row. Dec 1 st at same edge every other row once—13 (15—16) sts. Work even until armhole measures 5½″ (6″—6½″), end at front edge. Bind off 6 (6—5) sts at beg of next row. Work even 1 row. Dec 1 st at same edge of next row. Work even until armhole measures 8½″ (9″—9½″), end at side edge. Bind off 3 (4—5) sts every other row twice. Mark center edge for placement of 5 buttons.

LEFT FRONT: Work as for right front, reversing all shaping, and make 5 buttonholes along center edge opposite markers as follows: Starting at front edge work first stitch, bind off 2 stitches, work to end of row. On the next row, cast on 2 sts over those bound off.

HOOD: Cast on 10 sts. Working in stockinette st for 2 rows, cast on 10 sts at end of next 2 rows. Work even for 10″. Bind off 10 sts at beg of next 2 rows. Work even for 7″. Bind off.

FINISHING: Sew bound-off edges to back section to form hood. Sew shoulder, side, and sleeve seams of sweater. Set in sleeves. Sew hood to neck of sweater. With right side facing, work 1 row sl st around outer edges of sweater and work 1 row sc along front edge of hood. Sew ribbon to wrong sides of front edges, making slits for buttonholes. Sew on buttons. Make a chain 30″ long. Weave chain between sc along edge of hood and tie in bow under chin.

18

BIG PURPLE SWEATER

WINTER SWEATERS • EASY

Another winter monster, this one is guaranteed to provide warmth, sturdiness, and—if you make it in this color—attention in a crowd.

Sizes: Men's small (medium—large).

Materials: Mexiskeins Fine, color #42, maximilian purple, 1½ (1¾—2) pounds. Knitting needles, #10.

Gauge: 3 stitches = 1″; 5 rows = 1″.

Pattern (multiple of 10 stitches): Rows 1, 2, 3: K (row 1 is wrong side). Row 4: P 5, k 5. Row 5: P 4, *k 5, p 5, repeat from *, end p 1. Row 6: K 2, *p 5, k 5, repeat from *, end k 3. Row 7: P 4, *k 5, p 5, repeat from *, end p 1. Row 8: K 2, *p 5, k 5, repeat from *, end k 3. Row 9: P 2, *k 5, p 5, repeat from *, end p 3. Row 10: K 4, *p 5, k 5, repeat from *, end k 1. Row 11: K 5, p 5. Row 12: Repeat row 10. Row 13: Repeat row 9. Row 14: Repeat row 8. Row 15: Repeat row 7. Row 16: Repeat row 4. Garter stitch around edges.

PHOTOGRAPHS OF THE BIG PURPLE SWEATER AP-PEAR ON THE FRONT COVER AND ON THE LAST PAGE OF THE COLOR SECTION.

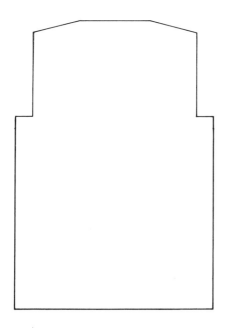

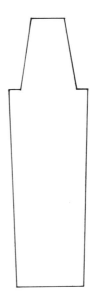

BACK: Cast on 58 (64—70) sts. Work in garter st for 1″. Establish pattern as follows: Rows 1, 2, 3: K. Row 4: K 4 (2—0), work row 1 of pattern to last 4 (2—0) sts, k 4 (2—0). Keeping first and last 4 (2—0) sts in reverse stockinette st (k on wrong side, p on right side) work even in pattern until piece measures 15″ (15½″—16″). Bind off 3 sts at beg of next 2 rows. Dec 1 st each end every other row 3 (4—5) times—46 (50—54) sts. Work even until armholes measure 8½″ (9″—9½″), ending with wrong side row. Working in garter st, bind off 3 (4—4) sts at beg of next 4 rows, 3 (3—5) sts at beg of next 2 rows. Bind off remaining 28 sts.

FRONT: Work same as back.

SLEEVES: Cast on 30 sts. Work in garter st for 1″. Working in pattern, inc 1 st each end every 1½″ (1½″—1¼″) 8 (9—11) times—46 (48—52) sts. Work even until piece measures 18½″ (19″—19½″). Bind off 3 sts at beg of next 2 rows. Dec 1 st each end every other row 15 (16—17) times. Bind off remaining 10 (10—12) sts.

FINISHING: Sew shoulder, side, and sleeve seams. Set in sleeves.

19

YELLOW, CREAM, AND BROWN SWEATER

WINTER SWEATERS • EASY

The brown stripes on the upper sleeves of this sweater came about because I ran out of yellow yarn just before I started the cap. Of course, this will never happen to you, but if it ever happens to a friend, you can tell her how successful this technique is.

Sizes: Women's small (medium—large).

Materials: Berga/Ullman's Hargarn, 3½ (4—4½) skeins cream (1192), 3½ (4—4½) skeins yellow (1378), 1 (1¼—1¼) skein brown (1756). Knitting needles, #5.

Gauge: 3½ stitches = 1″; 3½ rows = 1″.

Pattern: Seed stitch for body of sweater, alternating 2 rows of yellow and 2 rows of cream. Garter stitch at bottom—front, back, sleeves—and around neck.

A PHOTOGRAPH OF THE YELLOW, CREAM, AND BROWN SWEATER APPEARS ON PAGE 3 OF THE COLOR SECTION.

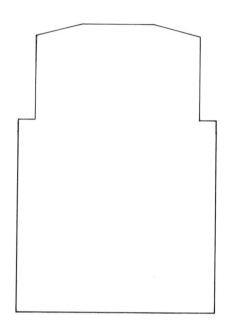

second ball of yarn, work in pattern across last 8 (11—14) sts. Working center 28 sts in garter st, work even for 1″. Bind off center 20 sts. Keeping 4 sts at each side of neck in brown garter st, work even until armholes measure 7½″ (8″—8½″). Bind off 4 (5—6) sts at beg of next 6 rows.

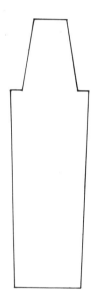

BACK: With brown, cast on 62 (68—74) sts. Work in garter st for 1″. Change to yellow. Work even in pattern until piece measures 14″. Bind off 5 sts at beg of next 2 rows. Dec 1 st each end every other row 4 times—44 (50—56) sts. Work even until armholes measure 7½″ (8″—8½″). Bind off 4 (5—6) sts at beg of next 6 rows—20 sts. Change to brown. Work in garter st for 1″. Bind off.

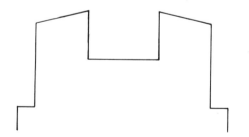

SLEEVES: With brown, cast on 30 sts. Work in garter st for 1″. Change to yellow. Working in pattern, inc 1 st each end every 2″ 6 (8—9) times—42 (46—48) sts. Work even until piece measures 17″ (17½″—18″). Change to brown. Work in brown for 1″. Change to yellow and continue in pattern. Bind off 5 sts at beg of next 2 rows. Dec 1 st each end every other row 11 (12—13) times. Bind off remaining 10 (12—12) sts.

FRONT: Work as for back until armholes measure 4¾″ (5¼″—5¾″). Work in pattern across first 8 (11—14) sts, attach brown, with brown k 28, attach

FINISHING: Sew shoulder, side, and sleeve seams. Set in sleeves.

20

GREEN, TAN, AND YELLOW V-NECK

WINTER SWEATERS • MEDIUM

This is a dense, heavy sweater because of the slip stitches. You can follow the color patterns given here, or invent one of your own. Sometimes it's nice to make up your own color variations as you go along. It requires a different kind of attention than just following a pattern and is often more pleasant to do.

Sizes: Men's small (medium—large).

Materials: Reynolds' Lopi, 6 (7—8) skeins of dark green (7375), 2 (3—4) skeins each of tan (7353A) and gold (7377). Knitting needles, #8 and #6. Aluminum crochet hook, size J.

Gauge: 4½ stitches = 1″; 6 rows = 1″.

Pattern (even number of stitches): Row 1: K 1, sl 1 with yarn in back. Row 2: Sl 1 with yarn in front, p 1. K 1, p 1 ribbing.

Color Pattern: This is the pattern from the bottom of the sweater: 8 rows green, 4 rows yellow, 4 rows green, 4 rows tan, 12 rows green, 2 rows tan, 8 rows yellow, 6 rows tan, 2 rows green, 4 rows yellow, 4 rows tan, 20 rows green, 2 rows yellow, 2 rows tan, 2 rows yellow, 2 rows tan, 4 rows yellow, 2 rows green, 4 rows tan, 12 rows green, 4 rows tan, 4 rows green, 2 rows yellow, 10 rows green. If sweater is longer than number of pattern rows, begin again with 9th row.

A PHOTOGRAPH OF THE GREEN, TAN, AND YELLOW V-NECK APPEARS ON PAGE 2 OF THE COLOR SECTION.

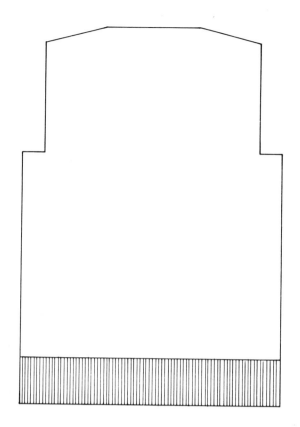

across first 32 (36—39) sts, k 2 tog, attach second ball of yarn, k 2 tog, work across remaining 32 (36—39) sts. Working on both sides at once, dec 1 st at each neck edge every other row 11 (12—12) times—21 (24—27) sts on each side. Work even until armholes measure 8½″ (9″—9½″). Bind off 7 (8—9) sts at beg of next 6 rows.

BACK: Using smaller needles, cast on 86 (96—104) sts. Work in k 1, p 1 ribbing for 3″. Change to larger needles. Work even in pattern until piece measures 13″. Bind off 5 sts at beg of next 2 rows. Dec 1 st each end every other row 4 (5—6) times—68 (76—82) sts. Work even until armholes measure 8½″ (9″—9½″). Bind off 7 (8—9) sts at beg of next 6 rows. Bind off remaining 26 (28—28) sts.

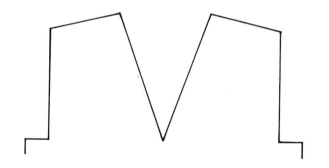

FRONT: Work as for back until armhole shaping is completed, ending with a wrong side row. Work

SLEEVES: Using smaller needles, cast on 42 (42—44) sts. Work in k 1, p 1 ribbing for 2″. Change to larger needles. Working in pattern, inc 1 st every ¾″ 13 (15—17) times—68 (72—78) sts. Work even until piece measures 18½″ (19″—19½″). Bind off 5 sts at beg of next 2 rows. Dec 1 st each end every other row 22 (23—25) times. Bind off remaining 14 (16—18) sts.

FINISHING: Sew shoulder, side, and sleeve seams. Set in sleeves. With right side facing, work 1 row sc around neck edge.

GRAY CREW NECK

WINTER SWEATERS • MEDIUM

The classic crew neck is here given a little extra charge with my favorite twist stitch and a couple of strategic slips. Easy and fast.

Sizes: Men's small (medium—large).

Materials: Bucilla's Wool and Shetland Wool, 12 (13—14) skeins Oxford gray (703). Knitting needles, #8 and #6.

Gauge: Yarn is worked double throughout. Stockinette stitch: 3 stitches = 1″; 5 rows = 1″. Twist and slipstitch: 4 stitches = 1″.

Pattern (multiple of 26 stitches): Row 1 (right side): P 5, (skip 1, k 1, k skipped stitch) twice, p 5, skip 1, k 1, k skipped stitch, p 3, skip 1, k 1, k skipped stitch, end p 5. Row 2: K 5, *p 2, k 3, p 2, k 5, p 4, k 5, repeat from * across. Row 3: P 5, *sl 4 with yarn in back, p 5, sl 2 with yarn in back, p 3, sl 2 with yarn in back, repeat from * across, end p 5. Row 4: K 5, *sl 2 with yarn in front, k 3, sl 2 with yarn in front, k 5, sl 4 with yarn in front, k 5, repeat from *. K 1, p 1 ribbing.

A PHOTOGRAPH OF THE GRAY CREW NECK APPEARS ON THE NEXT-TO-LAST PAGE OF THE COLOR SECTION.

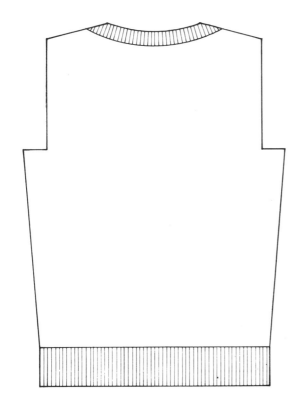

Attach second ball of yarn. Working on both sides at once, dec 1 st at each neck edge every other row 3 times—10 (12—14) sts on each side. Work even until armholes measure 8½″ (9″—9½″). Bind off 5 (6—7) sts at beg of next 4 rows.

BACK: Cast on 58 (64—70) sts. Work k 1, p 1 ribbing for 2½″. Change to larger needles. Establish pattern as follows: Row 1: P 3 (6—9), work row 1 of pattern to last 3 (6—9) sts, p 3 (6—9). Working center 52 sts in pattern and 3 (6—9) sts at each side in reverse stockinette st, work even until piece measures 15″. Bind off 3 sts at beg of next 2 rows. Dec 1 st each end every other row 3 (4—5) times—46 (50—54) sts. Work even until armholes measure 8½″ (9″—9½″). Bind off 5 (6—7) sts at beg of next 4 rows. Bind off remaining 26 sts.

SLEEVES: Cast on 26 sts. Work k 1, p 1 ribbing for 2½″. Change to larger needles. Working in pattern, inc 1 st each end every 1″ 10 (11—13) times—46 (48—52) sts. Work even until piece measures 18½″ (19″—19½″). Bind off 3 sts at beg of next 2 rows. Dec 1 st each end every other row 16 (17—18) times. Bind off remaining 8 (8—10) sts.

FINISHING: Block sweater pieces. Sew left shoulder seam. With right side facing, pick up and k 70 sts along neck edge. Work k 1, p 1 ribbing for 1″. Bind off in ribbing. Sew right shoulder and neckband seam. Sew underarm and sleeve seams. Set in sleeves.

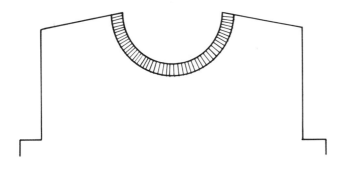

FRONT: Work same as back until armholes measure 5½″ (6″—6½″). Place center 20 sts on holder.

ROSE-COLORED BUMPY STITCH PULLOVER

WINTER SWEATERS • MEDIUM

My Aunt Shirley, who knit this one, didn't think it was a particularly quick stitch. I knit a sweater with it a couple of years ago and was amazed at how quickly it progressed. You'll just have to try it and see for yourself. The texture is wonderful and works just as well in a sport yarn as in this knitting worsted.

Sizes: Women's small (medium—large).

Materials: Spinnerin's Marvel-Twist Deluxe Knitting Worsted, 3½ (4—4½) skeins American Beauty (462). Knitting needles, #7. Aluminum crochet hook, size G.

Gauge: 6½ stitches = 1″; 6 rows = 1″.

Pattern (multiple of 4 stitches): Row 1 (wrong side): K 1, p 1, k 1 in same stitch, p 3 tog. Row 2: P. Row 3: P 3 tog, k 1, p 1, k 1 in same stitch. Row 4: P.

A PHOTOGRAPH OF THE ROSE-COLORED BUMPY STITCH PULLOVER APPEARS ON PAGE 5 OF THE COLOR SECTION.

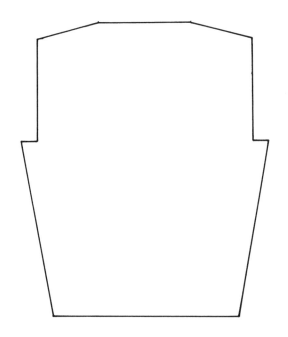

second ball of yarn. Working on both sides at once, dec 1 st at each neck edge every row 11 (13—15) times. Work even until armholes measure 7½″ (8″—8½″). Bind off 5 (6—7) sts at beg of next 6 rows.

BACK: Cast on 84 (92—100) sts. Working in pattern, inc 1 st each end every ½″ 14 (16—18) times —112 (124—136) sts. Work even until piece measures 8″ (8″—8½″). Bind off 7 (8—9) sts at beg of next 2 rows. Dec 1 st each end every other row 8 times—82 (92—102) sts. Work even until armholes measure 7½″ (8″—8½″). Bind off 5 (6—7) sts at beg of next 6 rows. Bind off remaining 52 (56—60) sts.

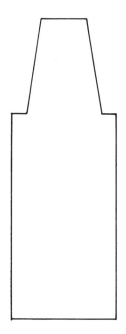

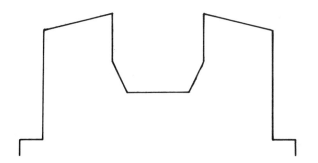

FRONT: Work same as back until armholes measure 3″ (3½″—4″). Bind off center 30 sts. Attach

SLEEVES: Cast on 76 (84—92) sts. Work even in pattern until piece measures 6″. Bind off 7 (8—9) sts at beg of next 2 rows. Dec 1 st each end every other row 20 (22—24) times. Bind off remaining 22 (24—26) sts.

FINISHING: Sew shoulder, side, and sleeve seams. Set in sleeves. With right side facing, work 1 row sc around all edges.

23

HEAVY BLACK AND WHITE TURTLENECK

WINTER SWEATERS • MEDIUM

Make no mistake about it, this is a heavy sweater. But Yvonne Malyack, who knit it, turned it out in a day. (She did complain about sore fingers, so maybe you should give it a week.)

Sizes: Men's small (medium—large).

Materials: Tahki's Greek Handspun Sheepswool, 1 (1½—2) pound black (101, color A) and ¼ (¾—1¼) pound white (105, color B). Knitting needles, #13, 4 double-pointed needles or circular knitting needle, #11.

Gauge: 4¼ stitches = 2″; 3 rows = 1″.

Pattern (multiple of 6 stitches plus 5): Row 1 (right side): With A, k.
Row 2: With A, k 1, p to last st, k 1.
Row 3: With B, k 1, *k 4, sl 2 with yarn in back, repeat from *, end k 4.
Row 4: With B, *k 4, sl 2 with yarn in front, repeat from *, end k 5.
Row 5: With A, k 3, *sl 2 with yarn in back, k 4, repeat from *, end sl 1, k 1.
Row 6: With A, k 1, sl 1 with yarn in front, *p 4, sl 2 with yarn in front, repeat from *, end p 2, k 1.
Row 7: With B, k 1, *sl 2 with yarn in back, k 4, repeat from *, end sl 2, k 2.
Row 8: With B, k 2, *sl 2 with yarn in front, k 4, repeat from *, end sl 2, k 1.
Rows 9 and 10: With A, repeat rows 1 and 2.
Row 11: With B, *k 4, sl 2 with yarn in back, repeat from *, end k 5.
Row 12: With B, k 5, *sl 2 with yarn in front, k 4, repeat from *.
Row 13: With A, k 1, sl 1 with yarn in back, *k 4, sl 2 with yarn in back, repeat from *, end k 3.
Row 14: With A, k 1, p 2, *sl 2 with yarn in front, p 4, repeat from *, end sl 1, k 1.
Row 15: With B, k 2, *sl 2 with yarn in back, k 4, repeat from *, end sl 2, k 1.
Row 16: With B, k 1, *sl 2 with yarn in front, k 4, repeat from *, end sl 2, k 2.

A PHOTOGRAPH OF THE HEAVY BLACK AND WHITE TURTLENECK APPEARS ON PAGE 3 OF THE COLOR SECTION.

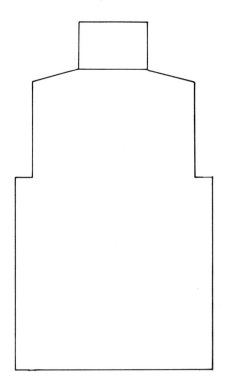

FRONT: Work same as back until armholes measure 5½" (6"—6½"). Place center 9 sts on holder, attach second ball of yarn and, working on both sides at once, dec 1 st at neck edge every other row twice. Work even until armholes measure 8½" (9"—9½"). Bind off 4 (5—6) sts at beg of next 4 rows.

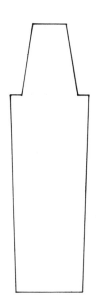

BACK: Using larger needles, cast on 35 (41—47) sts. Work even in pattern for 15½" (16"—16"). Bind off 2 sts at beg of next 2 rows. Dec 1 st each end every other row 1 (2—3) times—29 (33—37) sts. Work even until armholes measure 8½" (9"—9½"). Bind off 4 (5—6) sts at beg of next 4 rows. Place remaining 13 sts on holder.

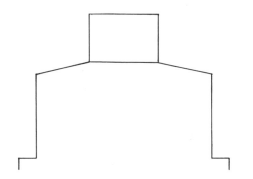

SLEEVES: Using larger needles, cast on 18 sts. Working in pattern, inc 1 st each end every 2" 6 (7—8) times—30 (32—34) sts. Work even until piece measures 18½" (19"—19½"). Bind off 1 st at beg of next 2 rows. Dec 1 st each end every other row 11 (12—13) times. Bind off remaining 6 sts.

FINISHING: Sew shoulder, side, and sleeve seams. Set in sleeves. With right side facing, using dp needles or circular needle and A, pick up and k 48 sts along neck edge, including sts on holders. Work in k 1, p 1 ribbing for 5". Bind off in ribbing.

24

SUNSHINE CAPE

WINTER SWEATERS • MEDIUM

This dramatic cape with its own sunbeams is perfect protection from winter winds. Just working on it is warming.

Sizes: Women's—one size fits all.

Materials: Mexiskeins fine, 2 skeins cream (#2), 3 skeins orange (#24), 2 skeins yellow (#10). Knitting needles, #10 and one #10 39″ circular knitting needle. Aluminum crochet hook, size G.

Gauge: 4 stitches = 1″; 5 rows = 1″.

Pattern: Seed stitch and stockinette stitch, as indicated. Work back and forth in rows on circular needle.

PHOTOGRAPHS OF THE SUNSHINE CAPE APPEAR ON THE BACK COVER AND ON PAGE 3 OF THE COLOR SECTION.

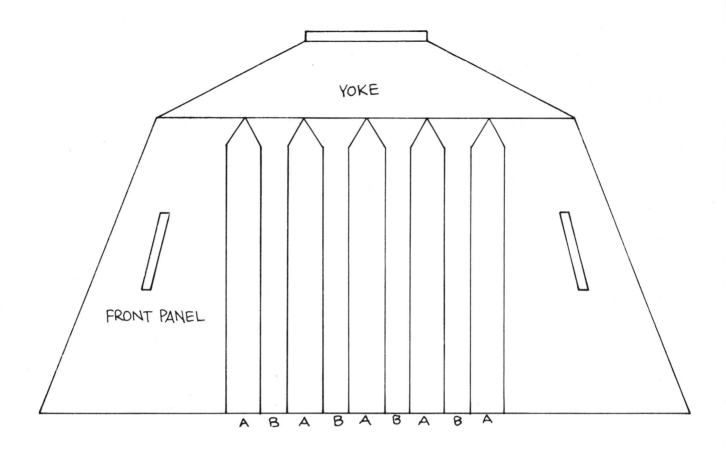

YOKE: With circular needle and yellow, cast on 42 sts. Working in stockinette st, work even for 1″, ending with a k row. Remainder of yoke is worked in reverse stockinette stitch. First inc row: *K 1, inc 1 in next st, repeat from *—63 sts. Work even for 2″, ending with a p row. Second inc row: K 1, *inc in next st, k 1, repeat from *—94 sts. Work even for 2″, ending with a p row. Third inc row: Repeat first inc row—141 sts. Work even until piece measures 8″. Bind off.

FRONT PANEL (make 2): With orange, cast on 30 sts. Working in stockinette st, dec 1 st at side edge every other row 5 times—25 sts. Inc 1 st at center front edge every other row 10 times—35 sts, ending at side edge. To shape arm opening—Next row: Work across first 17 sts, attach second ball of yarn and work across remaining 18 sts. Working on both sides at once, work even for 7½″, ending at side edge. Next row: Work across entire row with first ball, fastening off second ball. At the same time,

inc 1 st at center front edge every fourth row 20 times—55 sts, then work even until piece measures 26″. Bind off.

BACK INSERTS A (make 5): With cream, cast on 1 st. Working in seed st, inc 1 st each end every other row 5 times—11 sts. Work even until piece measures 26″. Bind off.

BACK STRIPS B (make 4): With orange, cast on 19 sts. Working in stockinette st, dec 1 st each end every other row 5 times—9 sts. Work even until piece measures 26″. Bind off.

FINISHING: Block pieces. Sew pieces together as shown in diagram. With right side facing, with orange work 1 row sc around outer edges and around arm openings. Ties (make 2): With orange, sl st at upper front corner, make a chain 8″ long, sl st in second ch from hook and in each ch across, fasten off. Tie in bow at center front.

25

YELLOW, BLUE, AND MAGENTA CROCHETED CARDIGAN

WINTER SWEATERS • MEDIUM

Another heavy, very warm jacket. The dynamic color pattern for this one can be adapted and used for any number of other sweaters, dresses, jackets, etc.

PHOTOGRAPHS OF THE YELLOW, BLUE, AND MAGENTA CROCHETED CARDIGAN APPEAR ON THE BACK COVER AND ON PAGE 2 OF THE COLOR SECTION.

Sizes: Women's small (medium—large).

Materials: Tahki's Heavy Handspun Sheepswool, 1 (1—1) skein magenta (706), 1½ (2—2½) pounds each blue (711) and yellow (701). Aluminum crochet hook, size K. Lining fabric, if desired.

Gauge: 2½ stitches = 1″; 3 rows = 1″.

Pattern: Single crochet.

Color Pattern: Follow graphs.

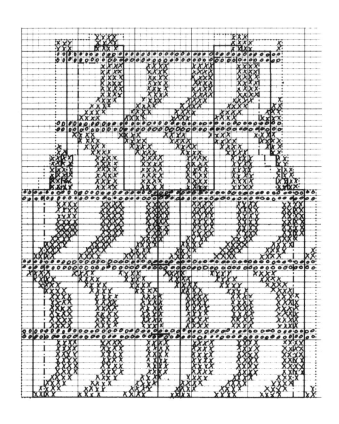

Work even until armholes measure 7½″ (8″—8½″). Sl st across first 4 (5—6) sc, work to last 4 (5—6) sc, turn. Repeat last row. Fasten off.

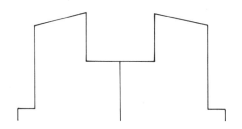

LEFT FRONT: With blue, ch 25 (27—29) sts. Following chart for colors, work even on 24 (26—28) sts until third magenta stripe has been completed. Sl st across first 3 sts, work to last 10 sts (neck edge). Working even at neck edge, dec 1 st at arm edge every other row 3 times—8 (10—12) sts. Work even until armhole measures 7½″ (8″—8½″), ending at arm edge. Sl st across first 4 (5—6) sc, work across row. Work across next row to last 4 (5—6) sc. Fasten off.

RIGHT FRONT: Work as for left front, working 3 buttonholes on magenta stripes as follows: Ch 3, skip next 3 sc. On the following row work 1 sc in each ch.

BACK: With blue, ch 45 (49—53) sts. Row 1: Following chart for colors, work 1 sc in second ch from hook and in each ch across—44 (48—52) sc. Row 2: Ch 1, turn, 1 sc in each sc across. Repeating row 2, work even until third magenta stripe has been completed. Sl st across first 3 sts, work to last 3 sts. Dec 1 sc every other row 3 times—32 (36—40) sts.

X = yellow
☐ = blue
O = magenta

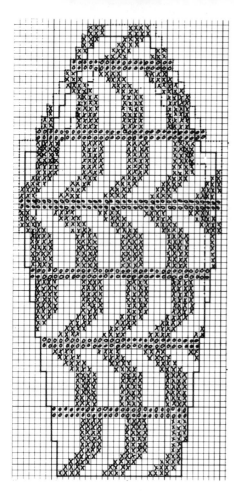

SLEEVES: With blue, ch 23 sts. Following chart, inc 1 st every 2" 4 (6—7) times—30 (34—36) sts. Work even until piece measures 18" (18½"—19"). Sl st across first 3 sts, work to last 3 sts, dec 1 st each end every other row 8 (9—9) times—8 (10—12) sts. Fasten off.

FINISHING: Sew shoulder, side, and sleeve seams. Set in sleeves. BUTTONS: With yellow, make 3. See p. 11 for instructions.

If lining is desired, cut lining fabric following sweater pieces for pattern, adding ½" seam allowance all around, before sewing sweater pieces together. Sew shoulder, side, and sleeve seams of lining. Set in sleeves. Turn under raw edges ½" and sew to edges of sweater.

26

HOODED TURTLE- NECK WITH GLOVES KNIT ON

WINTER SWEATERS •ADVANCED

This is an extremely practical sweater for small children and all the rest of us who find scarves, hats, and gloves too much to keep track of during the winter. Here's everything you need to face the cold, all in one piece. The instructions may appear wordy, but they're not at all difficult. Sit down and read them through first (you always do that anyway, don't you?) and you'll get a clear picture of what goes on.

These instructions are for yarn worked double, which makes a warm sweater, suitable for skiing, skating, sledding, snowball fights, and other enjoyable winter sports. Instructions for the gloves are given with one strand for a slightly less Abominable Snowman look about the hands than those shown in the photograph.

PHOTOGRAPHS OF THE HOODED TURTLENECK WITH GLOVES KNIT ON APPEAR ON PAGE 6 OF THE COLOR SECTION.

Sizes: Children's small (medium—large/women's small—medium—large).

Materials: Tahki's Donegal tweed, heavyweight, 6 (7—8) skeins of #816, green tweed (color A) and 2½ (3—3½) skeins of #824, chartreuse (color B) for women's sizes; 3 (4—5) skeins A and 1 (2—2) skeins B for children's sizes. This is a wonderful yarn, and I recommend it highly. Knitting needles, #7 and #5. Aluminum crochet hook, size E.

Gauge: 3 stitches = 1″; 5 rows = 1″ (with yarn worked double).

Pattern: K 1, p 1 ribbing; stockinette stitch.

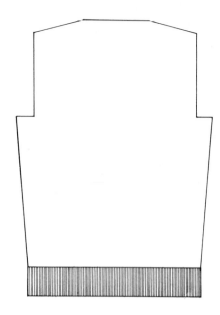

BACK: With smaller needles and double strand of A, cast on 34 (38—44/44—50—56) sts. Work in k 1, p 1 ribbing for 2½". Change to larger needles. Working in stockinette st, inc 1 st each end every 2" 2 (2—2/4—4—4) times. Work even on 38 (42—48/52—58—64) sts until piece measures 10" (10"—11"/11"—12"—12"). Bind off 2 (2—2/3—3—3) sts at beg of next 2 rows. Dec 1 st each end every other row 1 (2—4/4—5—6) times—32 (34—36/38—42—46) sts. Work even until armholes measure 4¾" (5"—6¼"/7½"—8"—8½"). Bind off 3 (4—4/4—4—5) sts at beg of next 4 rows, 4 (3—3/4—5—5) sts at beg of next 2 rows. Place remaining 12 (12—14/14—16—16) sts on holder.

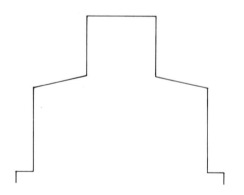

FRONT: Work same as back until armholes measure 2¼" (2½"—3¾"/4½"—5"—5½"). Place center 8 (8—10/10—12—12) sts on holder. Attach second ball of yarn. Working on both sides at once, at each neck edge dec 1 st every other row twice—10 (11—11/12—13—15) sts on each side. Work even until armholes measure 4¾" (5"—6¼"/7½"—8"—8½"). Bind off 3 (4—4/4—4—5) sts at beg of next 4 rows, 4 (3—3/4—5—5) sts at beg of next 2 rows.

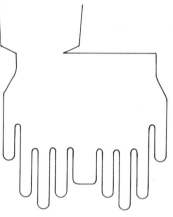

LEFT GLOVE AND SLEEVE: Half Thumb (make 2)—With smaller needles and single strand of B, cast on 2 (3—3/4—4—4) sts. Working in stockinette st, inc 1 st each end on second row, then work even until piece measures 1½" (1½"—2½"/2½"—2½"—3"). Break off. Place thumbs on one holder. Half Fingers (make 6)—Cast on 1 (1—2/3—3—4) sts. Inc 1 st each end of second row, then work even until piece measures 2" (2½"—3"/3½"—3¾"—4"). Break off. Place fingers on second holder. Pinkie (make 1)—Cast on 2 (2—3/6—6—7) sts. Inc 4 sts on second row, then work even until piece measures 2" (2¼"—2¼"/2½"—2½"—3"). Break off but leave on needle. Palm—Slip 3 half fingers on to needle, work across sts of 3 half fingers, sts of pinkie, slip other 3 half fingers on to needle and work across these—24 (24—31/40—40—47) sts. Work even for 1" (1"—1"/1½"—1½"—1½"). Break off. Slip 1 half thumb to needle, work across sts of 1 half thumb, work across sts of palm, slip other half thumb onto needle, work across sts of other half thumb—32 (34—41/52—52—59) sts. Work for 1½" (1½"—1½"/2"—2"—2"), decreasing 0 (0—0/1—1—1) st every other row 0 (0—0/

5—5—5) times. Work in k 1, p 1 ribbing for 1", ending with wrong side row. Bind off first 20 (22—29/30—35—42) sts. Using double strand of A, work across remaining 12 sts. Cast on 8 (8—10/10—12—14) sts—20 (20—22/22—24—26) sts. Work in k 1, p 1 ribbing for 1½", ending with a wrong side row. Change to larger needles. Working in stockinette st, inc 1 st every 2" 4 (6—7/8—8—8) times—28 (32—36/38—40—42) sts. Work even until sleeve measures 11" (13"—14"/18"—18½"—19"). Bind off 3 (4—4/4—4—5) sts at beg of next 2 rows. Dec 1 st each end every other row 9 (10—12/13—14—14) times. Bind off remaining 4 sts.

RIGHT GLOVE AND SLEEVE: Work same as left glove through 1" of ribbing, ending with a right side row. Complete as for left glove and sleeve.

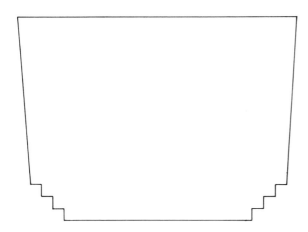

HOOD: With larger needles and double strand of B, pick up 32 (32—32/36—36—36) sts along sides and back of neck. Work even in stockinette st for 1". On next row and every other row inc 5 (5—5/6—6—6) sts evenly spaced, 3 times—47 (47—47/54—54—54) sts. Work even until piece measures 13" (13"—13/14"—14"—14"). Divide sts evenly on 2 needles and weave edges together. With right side facing and double strand of B, work 1 row sc along edge of hood. With double strand of B, make a chain 40" long. Weave ends through scs. Tie in bow under chin.

FINISHING: Block sweater pieces. Sew left shoulder seam. With right side facing and double strand of A, pick up and k 34 (34—38/42—46—46) sts around neck edge. Work in k 1, p 1 ribbing for 5". Bind off in ribbing. Sew right shoulder, side and sleeve seams. Set in sleeves. Fold gloves in half and sew corresponding edges together. Fold turtleneck in half and tack down.

RAINBOW SWEATER

WINTER SWEATERS • ADVANCED

This sweater was the most complicated to figure out, but it is fairly simple to work. And so spectacular! Working on it is being surrounded by an explosion of color. It consists of ten pieces crocheted separately and then assembled: two central arches, two bottom arches, two side pieces, front top and back top, and two sleeves.

Sizes: Women's small (medium—large). Sizing adjustments made in side pieces, front top and back top, and sleeves.

Materials: Berga/Ullman's Ryagarn, 2 (2½—3) skeins of colors red (2059), orange (1758), yellow (1079), green (4248), blue (3058), violet (2737). The Ryagarn is rug yarn and bracingly scratchy: you'll probably want to line it. You *can* substitute any other yarn that will give the same gauge, but you won't get the same firmness or the same long-wearing qualities. Aluminum crochet hook, #7.

Gauge: Single crochet = 4 stitches per inch, 5 rows per inch; half double crochet = 3½ stitches per inch, 2½ rows per inch; double crochet = 3½ stitches per inch, 2 rows per inch.

Pattern: Single crochet; half double crochet; double crochet. For all color-change rows throughout sweater, work in back loop of sts only.

PHOTOGRAPHS OF THE RAINBOW SWEATER APPEAR ON THE BACK COVER AND ON THE LAST PAGE OF THE COLOR SECTION.

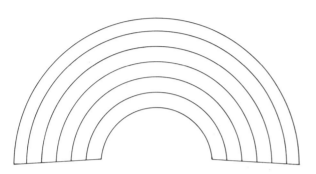

CENTRAL ARCH (make 2): With violet, chain 34. **Row 1:** Work in sc. Inc 1 sc in sts #8, 12, 20, 24 (36 sc). **Row 2:** Inc 1 sc at each end (38 sc). **Row 3:** Inc 1 sc in sts #9, 14, 24, 29 (42 sc). **Row 4:** Inc 1 st at each end (44 sc). Change to blue. **Row 5:** Inc 1 sc in sts #10, 18, 26, 34 (48 sc). **Row 6:** Inc 1 sc at each end (50 sc). **Row 7:** Inc 1 sc in sts #9, 17, 25, 33, 41 (55 sc). **Row 8:** Inc 1 sc at each end (57 sc). Change to green. **Row 9:** Inc 1 sc in sts #9, 17, 25, 33, 41, 49 (63 sc). **Row 10:** Inc 1 sc at each end (65 sc). **Row 11:** Inc 1 sc in sts #8, 16, 24, 32, 40, 48, 56 (72 sc). **Row 12:** Inc 1 sc at each end (74 sc). Change to yellow. **Row 13:** Inc 1 sc in sts #12, 22, 32, 42, 52, 62 (80 sc). **Row 14:** Inc 1 sc at each end (82 sc). **Row 15:** Inc 1 sc in sts #11, 23, 35, 47, 59, 61 (88 sc). **Row 16:** Work even. Change to orange. **Row 17:** Inc 1 sc in sts #14, 26, 38, 50, 62, 74 (94 sc). **Row 18:** Inc 1 sc at each end (96 sc). **Row 19:** Inc 1 sc in sts #17, 29, 41, 53, 65, 77 (102 sc). **Row 20:** Work even. Change to red. **Row 21:** Inc 1 sc in sts #21, 36, 51, 66, 81, 96 (108 sc). **Row 22:** Inc 1 sc at each end (110 sc). **Row 23:** Inc 1 sc in sts #18, 33, 48, 63, 78, 93 (116 sc). **Row 24:** Work even.

BOTTOM ARCH (fits upside down into open space at bottom of central arch. Make 2): With red, ch 5.

Row 1: Work in sc. Inc 1 sc in sts #2, 4 (7 sc). **Row 2:** Inc 1 sc at each end (9 sc). Change to orange. **Row 3:** Inc 1 sc in sts #3, 7 (11 sc). **Row 4:** Inc 1 sc at each end (13 sc). **Row 5:** Inc 1 sc in sts #5, 9 (15 sc). **Row 6:** Inc 1 sc at each end (17 sc). Change to green. **Row 7:** Inc 1 sc in sts #4, 7, 10, 13 (21 sc). **Row 8:** Work even. Change to blue. **Rows 9 and 10:** Work even. Change to violet. **Row 11:** Inc 1 sc in sts #4, 8, 14, 18 (25 sc). **Row 12:** Work even.

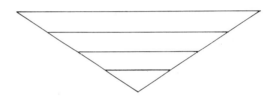

SIDE PIECE (fits between front central arch and back central arch, with point down. Top 16 sts of arch and tops of side piece make a straight line. Make 2): With red, ch 2. Work in sc, working 4 rows of each color in same order as for bottom arch. Inc 3 sc each end every other row 8 times; for medium size: in addition, inc 1 sc each end in rows 5 and 15, for large size inc additional sc each end in rows 4, 8, 12, and 16. Last row (row 16) will have 50 (54—58) sc. Sew side pieces to arches before continuing.

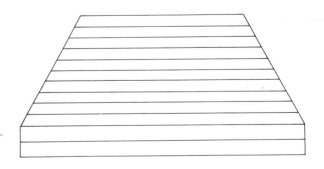

FRONT TOP AND BACK TOP (make 2 pieces): With orange, work hdc across the straight line made by top of arch and top of side pieces. Starting at center of one side piece, work across top of arch to center of second side piece—60 (64—68) hdc. Working 2 rows of each color, work even for 1" (1½"—2"). Continuing to work 2 rows of each color, dec 1 st each end every other row 10 (11—12) times.

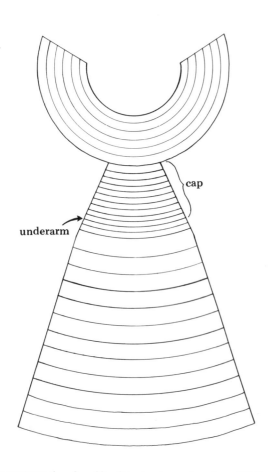

cap

underarm

SLEEVES (make 2): Start at neck edge. With red, ch 34. **Row 1:** Work in sc. Inc 1 sc in sts #8, 12, 20, 24 (36 sc). **Row 2:** Inc 1 sc at each end (38 sc). Change to orange. **Row 3:** Inc 1 sc in sts #9, 14, 24, 29 (42 sc). **Row 4:** Inc 1 sc at each end (44 sc).

Change to yellow. **Row 5:** Inc 1 sc in sts #10, 18, 26, 34 (48 sc). **Row 6:** Inc 1 sc at each end (50 sc). Change to green. **Row 7:** Inc 1 sc in sts #9, 17, 25, 33, 41 (55 sc). **Row 8:** Inc 1 sc at each end (57 sc). Change to blue. **Row 9:** Inc 1 sc in sts #9, 17, 25, 33, 41, 49 (63 sc). **Row 10:** Inc 1 sc at each end (65 sc).

Change to violet. **Row 11:** Inc 1 sc in sts #8, 16, 24, 32, 40, 48, 56 (72 sc). **Row 12:** Inc 1 sc at each end (74 sc). Begin sleeve cap: With red, work hdc in sts #31-43 (29-45—27-47) of last violet row. **Row 1:** Inc 1 hdc in sts #3, 11. **Row 2:** Work even —15 (19—23) hdc. Change to orange. **Row 3:** Inc 1 hdc in sts #2, 7, 13. **Row 4:** Work even—18 (22—26) hdc. Change to yellow. **Row 5:** Inc 1 hdc in sts #2, 8, 15. **Row 6:** Work even—21 (25—29) hdc. Change to green. **Row 7:** Inc 1 hdc in sts #2, 7, 12, 19. **Row 8:** Work even—25 (29—33) hdc. Change to blue. **Row 9:** Inc 1 hdc in sts #3, 9, 15, 21. **Row 10:** Work even—29 (33—37) hdc. Change to violet. **Row 11:** Inc 1 hdc in sts #3, 10, 17, 25. **Row 12:** Work even—33 (37—41) hdc. Change to red. **Row 13:** Inc 1 hdc in sts #8, 12, 20, 24. **Row 14:** Work even—37 (41—45) hdc. Change to orange. **Row 15:** Inc 1 hdc in sts #10, 15, 22, 27. **Row 16:** Work even—41 (45—49) hdc. Change to yellow. **Row 17:** Inc 1 hdc in sts #10, 16, 24, 32. **Row 18:** Work even—45 (49—53) hdc. Change to green. **Row 19:** Inc 1 hdc in sts #10, 18, 26, 34. **Row 20:** Work even—49 (53—57) hdc. (This is underarm.) Change to blue. **Row 21:** Inc 1 hdc in sts #8, 16, 24, 32, 40. **Row 22:** Dec 2 hdc at each end—50 (54—58) hdc. Change to violet. **Row 23:** Inc 1 hdc in sts #8, 16, 24, 32, 40. **Row 24:** Dec 3 hdc at each end —49 (53—57) hdc. Change to red. **Row 25:** Work in dc. Inc 1 dc in sts #8, 16, 24, 32, 40. **Row 26:** Dec 2 dc at each end—50 (54—58) dc. Change to orange. **Row 27:** Inc 1 dc in sts #9, 17, 25, 33, 41. **Row 28:** Dec 2 dc at each end—51 (55—59) dc. Change to yellow. **Row 29:** Inc 1 dc in sts #9, 17,

25, 33, 41. **Row 30:** Dec 2 dc at each end—52 (56—60) dc. Change to green. **Row 31:** Inc 1 dc in sts #10, 18, 26, 34, 42. **Row 32:** Dec 2 dc at each end—53 (57—61) dc. Change to blue. **Row 33:** Inc 1 dc in sts #10, 18, 26, 34, 42. **Row 34:** Dec 2 dc at each end—54 (58—62) dc. Change to violet. **Row 35:** Inc 1 dc in sts #11, 19, 27, 35, 43. **Row 36:** Dec 2 dc at each end—55 (59—63). Change to red. **Row 37:** Inc 1 dc in sts #11, 19, 27, 35, 43. **Row 38:** Dec 2 dc at each end—56 (60—64) dc. Change to orange. **Row 39:** Inc 1 dc in sts #12, 20, 28, 36, 44. **Row 40:** Dec 2 dc at each end—57 (61—65) dc.

Change to yellow. **Row 41:** Inc 1 dc in sts #8, 16, 24, 32, 40, 48. **Row 42:** Dec 3 dc at each end—57 (61—65) dc. Repeat rows 41 and 42 with rainbow sequence until sleeve is desired length.

FINISHING: Crochet 10 buttons in any color you wish. Sew sleeve seams to underarm. Sew small bottom arches, wide end up, into large central arches. Sew back to sleeve cap. Crochet loops for 5 buttons evenly spaced along front of each sleeve cap. Sew 5 buttons to each side of sweater to match button loops.

28

ANGORA V-NECK WITH FLOATING SLEEVES

EVENING/SOPHISTICATED SWEATERS • EASY

Working with angora is a strange experience: the yarn muffles the click of the needles the way a snowstorm muffles traffic noises. It makes the act of knitting seem slow and restrained. The floating sleeves give this sweater great sophistication and can be used to dress up any sweater.

Sizes: Women's small (medium—large).

Materials: Joseph Galler's 100% Angora, 16 (18—20) skeins Coral. Knitting needles, #5 and #3. Aluminum crochet hook, size E.

Gauge: Stockinette stitch, 4½ stitches = 1″; 5 rows = 1″. Lace stitch, 4 stitches = 1″; 6 rows = 1″.

Pattern: Lace stitch for sleeves and yoke (odd number of stitches): Row 1: K 1, *yo, k 2 tog, repeat from *. All even-numbered rows: P. Row 3: K. Row 5: K 2, *yo, k 2 tog, repeat from *, end k 1. Row 7: K. K 1, p 1 ribbing; stockinette stitch.

A PHOTOGRAPH OF THE ANGORA V-NECK WITH FLOATING SLEEVES APPEARS ON THE FIRST PAGE OF THE COLOR SECTION.

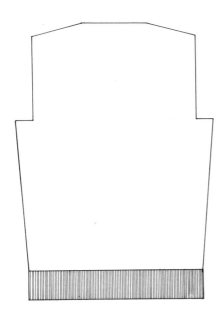

BACK: Using smaller needles, cast on 58 (64—68) sts. Work in k 1, p 1 ribbing for 2½". Change to larger needles. Working in stockinette st, inc 1 st each end every ½" 10 (12—14) times—78 (88—96) sts. Work even until piece measures 11". Bind off 5 sts at beg of next 2 rows. Dec 1 st each end every other row 5 (7—8) times—58 (64—70) sts. Work even until armholes measure 7½" (8"—8½"). Bind off 5 (6—7) sts at beg of next 6 rows. Bind off remaining 28 sts.

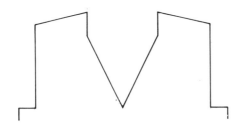

FRONT: Work same as back until piece measures 9", ending with a wrong side row. K 37 (42—46), k 2 tog, attach second ball of yarn, k 2 tog, k 37 (42—46). Working on both sides at once, dec 1 st at each neck edge every other row 13 (14—13) times and at the same time, when piece measures 11", bind off 5 sts at beg of next 2 rows, then dec 1 st each side edge every other row 5 (7—8) times —15 (17—21) sts on each side. Work even in pattern until armholes measure 7½" (8"—8½"). Bind off 5 (6—7) sts at beg of next 4 rows, 5 (5—7) sts at beg of next 2 rows.

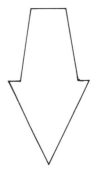

SLEEVES: Using larger needles, cast on 3 sts. Working in stockinette st for 2" and then in pattern, inc 1 st each end every row 26 (28—30) times —55 (59—63) sts. Work even for 1". Bind off 5 sts at beg of next 2 rows. Dec 1 st each end every other row 15 (16—17) times. Bind off remaining 15 (17—19) sts.

FINISHING: Block pieces. Sew shoulder, side, and sleeve seams. Set in sleeves. With right side facing, work 1 row sc around neck and sleeve edges.

29

RIBBON CAP SLEEVE V-NECK

EVENING/SOPHISTICATED SWEATERS • MEDIUM

Ribbon knits and cap sleeves, which were all the rage in the 1940s, have been unfashionable for a long time, but are making a return, along with everything else from the '40s. This is a lightweight, extremely elegant sweater, suitable for evening wear, and surprisingly inexpensive to make.

Sizes: Women's small (medium—large).

Materials: Fibre Yarn's #3 Braid, 2 (2½—3) spools color A (dark blue), 1 (1¼—1½) spool each color B (pale blue) and color C (tan). No substitutes. Knitting needles, #6. Aluminum crochet hook, size E.

Gauge: 4 stitches = 1″; 5 rows = 1″.

Pattern: Stockinette stitch with knit stitches worked in back of stitch.

A PHOTOGRAPH OF THE RIBBON CAP SLEEVE V-NECK APPEARS ON THE NEXT-TO-LAST PAGE OF THE COLOR SECTION.

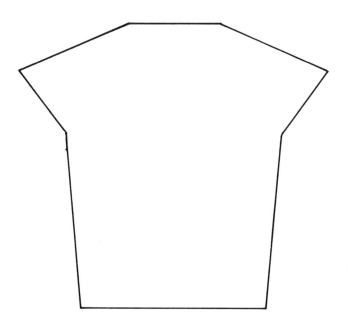

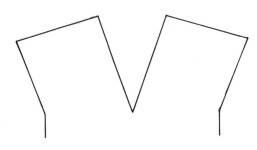

BACK: With A, cast on 68 (76—84) sts. Working in pattern, work 2 rows A, 10 rows B, 2 rows A, 10 rows C, then with A work even until piece measures 11″. Inc 1 st each end every row 14 (16—18) times. Continuing to inc 1 st each end every row, work next 4 incs with C, next 2 with A, and next 4 with B—forming stripes at ends of caps—24 (26—28) incs on each side, 116 (128—140) sts total. Bind off 6 (7—8) sts at beg of next 12 rows, 4 sts at beg of next 4 rows. Bind off remaining 28 sts.

FRONT: Work same as back until piece measures 10½″, ending with a wrong side row. Work across first 32 (36—40) sts, k 2 tog, attach second ball of yarn, k 2 tog, work across row. Working on both sides at once, dec 1 st at each neck edge every third row 13 times, and at the same time work cap sleeves and shoulders as for back, working even on neck edges until all shoulder sts have been bound off.

FINISHING: Sew left shoulder seam. With right side facing and B, pick up 109 (113—117) sts along neck edge including 1 st at center front. Working in pattern and decreasing 1 st each side of center front st every row, work 4 rows B, 2 rows C. Bind off. Sew right shoulder and side seams. With A, work 1 row sc around lower edge and sleeves. With C, work 1 row sc around neck.

30

RED AND WHITE RAYON EVENING JACKET

EVENING/SOPHISTICATED SWEATERS • MEDIUM

Rayon is a delight to work with. It slithers along most obediently and in this heavy weight really makes up quickly. If you drop stitches, they have a tendency to slide out of control, so be careful not to.

Sizes: Women's small (medium—large).

Materials: Golden Fleece's Xochitl, 100% rayon, 4 (5—6) skeins white (X16), 1 (1½—2) red (X10) for small woman's size. Knitting needles, #9. Aluminum crochet hook, size H. 4 1″ buttons.

Gauge: 4 stitches = 1″; 6 rows = 1″.

Pattern: Stockinette with twisted slip stitch ribs, placed as follows: two in back, where indicated in pattern; one up center of each front half and each sleeve. Make rib as follows: **Row 1:** K 2 tog, but leave on needle. Insert right-hand needle between the sts and k the first st. Slide new sts off needle. **Row 2:** Sl these 2 with yarn in front. **Row 3:** Sl these 2 with yarn in back. **Row 4:** P these 2. Repeat these 4 rows for rib.

Make all increases and decreases on right side of work, as follows: To increase, k in front and back of same stitch. To decrease before rib: sl 1, k 1, pass the sl st over the k st. To decrease after rib: k 2 tog.

Follow graph below for red triangle.

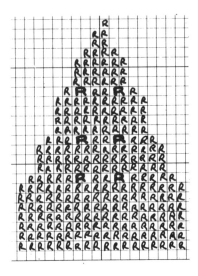

R =Red
R =Decrease, following pattern instructions.

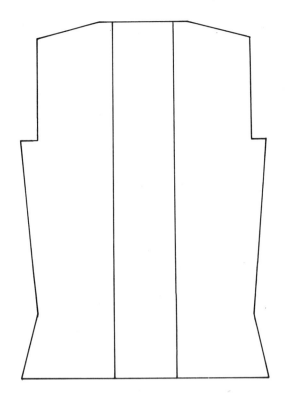

at st 8 (10—12). Work in red to st 15 (17—19), work row 1 of rib across next 2 sts, work in red for 8 more sts. Continue in white to end of row. Continuing in this manner, working triangle as shown in graph, dec 1 st each side of rib every 2″ 3 times, work even for 3″, inc 1 st at each side of rib every 2″ 3 times, then work even until piece measures 17″. At arm edge bind off 4 sts at beg of next row, dec 1 st every other row 5 (6—7) times, then work even. At the same time, when piece measures 14½″, shape lapel as follows: **Row 1** (right side): Work across to within 4 sts of center front edge, inc 1 st, p 3. **Row 2**: K 4, work across in pattern. Repeat this inc every other row 16 times, working each consecutive inc 1 st farther from outer edge, then dec 1 st every other row in same manner 17 times. At neck edge bind off 8 (8—9) sts once, then 7 (8—8) sts once, and at arm edge bind off 5 (6—7) sts every other row twice. Mark front edge for placement of 4 buttons, the first 1″ from lower edge and the last at beg of lapel shaping, the others evenly spaced between.

BACK: With white, cast on 68 (76—84) sts. **Row 1**: Work in white in stockinette st, begin red triangle at stitch 13 (17—21). Work in red to st 21 (25—29), work row 1 of rib across next 2 sts, work in red for 8 more sts. Work in white in stockinette for 6 sts. Start second triangle in red, working row 1 of rib at ninth and tenth sts. Work red for 8 more sts, continue with white to end of row. Continuing in pattern as established, and working triangle as shown in graph, dec 1 st each side of each rib every 2″ 3 times, work even for 3″, inc 1 st each side of each rib every 2″ 3 times, then work even until piece measures 17″. Bind off 4 sts at beg of next 2 rows. Dec 1 st each end every other row 5 (6—7) times—50 (56—62) sts. Work even until armholes measure 7½″ (8″—8½″). Bind off 5 (6—7) sts at beg of next 4 rows. Bind off remaining 30 (32—34) sts.

RIGHT FRONT: Work to correspond to left front, reversing all shaping and working 4 buttonholes opposite markers as follows: Starting at center front edge, work 3 sts, bind off next 3 sts, work across row. On the next row cast on 3 sts over those bound off.

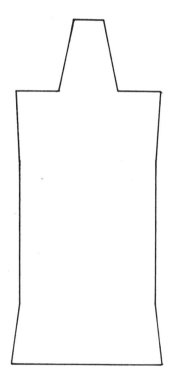

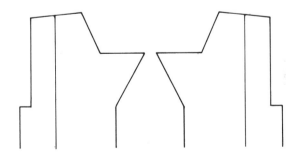

LEFT FRONT: Cast on 34 (38—42) sts. **Row 1**: Work in white in stockinette st. Begin red triangle

SLEEVES: Cast on 34 sts with white. **Row 1**: With white, k 12; with red, k 4, work rib over next 2 sts, k 4; with white, k 12. **Row 2**: With white, p 12;

with red, p 4, work rib, p 4; with white, p 12. **Rows 3 and 4:** Repeat rows 1 and 2. **Row 5:** With white, k 13; with red, k 3, work rib, k 3; with white, k 13. **Row 6:** With white, p 13; with red, p 3, work rib, p 3; with white, p 13. **Rows 7 and 8:** Repeat rows 5 and 6. **Row 9:** With white, k 14; with red, p 2, work rib, p 2; with white, k 14. **Row 10:** With white, p 14; with red, p 2, work rib, p 2; with white, p 14. **Rows 11 and 12:** Repeat rows 9 and 10. **Row 13:** With white, k 15; with red, k 1, work rib, k 1; with white, k 15. **Row 14:** With white, p 15; with red, p 1, work rib, p 1; with white, k 15. **Rows 15 and 16:** Repeat rows 13 and 14. **Row 17:** With white, k 16; with red, work rib; with white, k 16. **Row 18:** With white, p 16; with red, work rib; with white, p 16. **Rows 19 and 20:** Repeat rows 17 and 18. Continuing in pattern with white only, inc 1 st each end every 1″ 7 (9—11) times—48 (52—56) sts. Work even until sleeve measures 18″ (18½″—19″). Bind off 4 sts at beg of next 2 rows. Dec 1 st each end every other row 12 (14—16) times. Bind off remaining 16 sts.

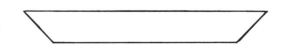

COLLAR: With red, cast on 60 (64—68) sts. Working in stockinette st, inc 1 st each end every other row until piece measures 4″. Bind off.

FINISHING: Block pieces. Sew shoulder, side, and sleeve seams. Set in sleeves. Work 1 row sc around edges. Sew on buttons.

31

CROCHET JUNGLE

KIDS' SWEATERS • MEDIUM

This miniature menagerie will delight any child. And, like all kids' sweaters, it's a pleasure to work because it goes so quickly.

Sizes: Children's small (medium—large).

Materials: Bucilla's Knitting Worsted, 1 (1—1 except where otherwise noted) skein each Orange (56) Apricot Brandy (91), (2—2) Green (80), (2—2) Green (95), (2—2) Green (97), Dark Oxford (70), Russet Brown (384), Gold (356), Antique Gold (358), Black (399), White (1). One aluminum crochet hook, size 10½.

Gauge: Yarn is worked double throughout. 3 stitches = 1″; 3½ rows = 1″.

Pattern: Single crochet.

Color Pattern: Follow graphs for placement of animals.

A PHOTOGRAPH OF THE CROCHET JUNGLE APPEARS ON PAGE 4 OF THE COLOR SECTION.

O = brown
X = black
/ = dark green
| = white
background = 1 strand light green and 1 strand
medium green worked together

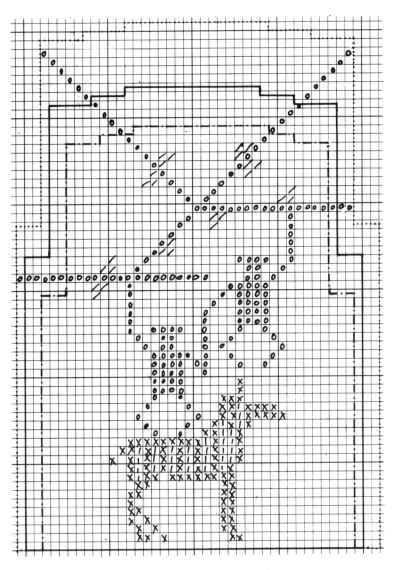

BACK: Ch 38 (41—44). Row 1: 1 sc in second ch from hook and in each remaining st of ch—37 (40—43) sc. Row 2: Ch 1, turn, 1 sc in each sc across. Repeating row 2 for pattern, work even until piece measures 9½" (11"—12"). Sl st across first 3 sts, 1 sc in each sc to last 3 sts—31 (34—37) sc. Work even until armholes measure 4¾" (5"—6¼"). Sl st across first 4 (5—5) sts, 1 sc in each sc to last 4 (5—5) sts. Sl st across first 4 (4—5) sts, 1 sc in each sc to last 4 (4—5) sts. Fasten off.

O = apricot brandy
X = orange
■ = black
    background = dark green

‑ = gray
| = white
■ = black
\\ = antique gold
G = gold
X = orange
    background = 1 strand light green and 1 strand
    medium green worked together

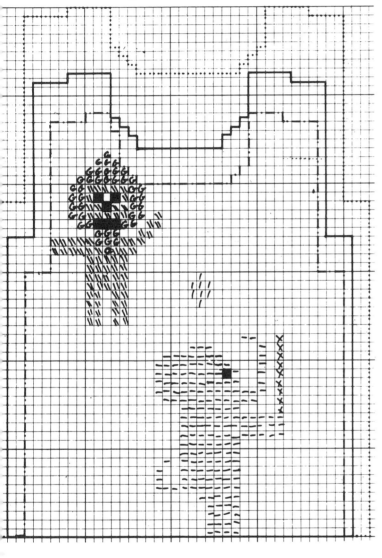

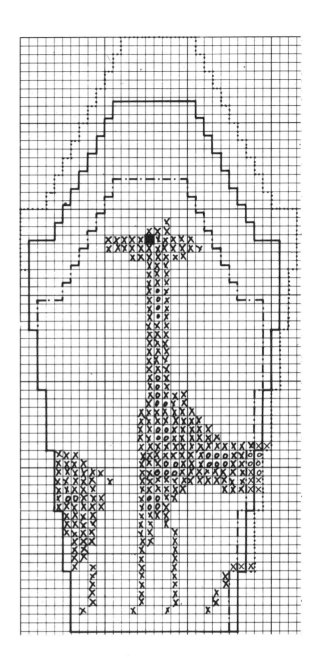

FRONT: Work same as back until armholes measure 2¾" (3"—4¼"). Work across first 11 (12—13) sts. Turn. Dec 1 st at neck edge every row 3 times—8 (9—10) sts. Work even until armholes measure 4¾" (5"—6¼"), ending at arm edge. Sl st across first 4 (5—5) sts, 1 sc in each sc across. Fasten off. Skip center 9 (10—11) sts for front of neck. Attach yarn and work other side to correspond, reversing all shaping.

SLEEVES: Ch 20 (21—22). Row 1: 1 sc in second ch from hook and in each remaining st of ch—19 (20—21) sc. Row 2: Ch 1, turn, 1 sc in each sc across. Repeating row 2 for pattern, inc 1 sc each end every 2" 4 (5—6) times—27 (30—33) sts. Work even until sleeves measure 11" (13"—14"). Sl st across first 3 sts, 1 sc in each sc to last 3 sts—21 (24—27) sts. Dec 1 st each end every other row 7 (8—9) times. Fasten off.

FINISHING: Sew shoulder, underarm, and sleeve seams. Set in sleeves.

32

BABY BUNTING

KIDS' SWEATERS • MEDIUM

Even the idea of a bunting is cozy and com-
forting. The instructions here are for a bunting
with sleeves, but you can always just make
the bunting wider and do away with the
sleeves altogether. The pattern allows room
for active kicking in the bottom. The mock
cable used here is a favorite stitch of mine.
It's simple to do and it looks good.

Sizes: Baby's small (medium—large).

Materials: Joseph Galler, Inc.'s 10 Little Indians yarn, 7 skeins. One pair #2 needles. One steel crochet hook, #0. One 14" zipper.

Gauge: 9 stitches = 1"; 8 rows = 1".

Pattern (multiple of 6 stitches): Row 1: K 2 tog, but leave on left-hand needle. Insert right-hand needle between the 2 sts, k the first st again, then slip both sts from the needle together, p 4. Row 2: K 4, p 2. Row 3: K 2, p 4. Row 4: K 4, p 2.

PHOTOGRAPHS OF THE BABY BUNTING APPEAR ON THE FIRST PAGE OF THE COLOR SECTION.

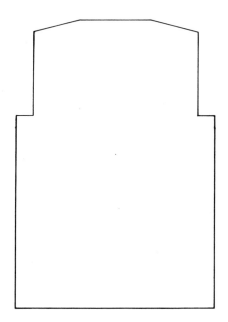

BACK: Cast on 96 (102—108) sts. Work even in pattern for 13¼" (14"—14¾"). Bind off 6 sts at beg of next 2 rows. Dec 1 st each end every other row 2 (3—5) times—80 (84—86) sts. Work even until armholes measure 3¾" (4"—4¼"). Bind off 6 (7—7) sts at beg of next 6 rows. Place remaining 44 (42—44) sts on holder.

SLEEVES: Cast on 48 sts. Work in k 1, p 1 ribbing for 2½". Working in pattern, inc 1 st each end every third (fourth—fifth) row 11 (12—13) times—70 (72—74) sts. Work even until sleeve measures 7½" (8"—8½"). Bind off 6 sts at beg of next 2 rows. Dec 1 st each end every row 20 (21—22) times. Bind off remaining 18 sts.

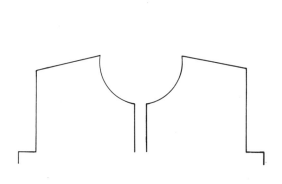

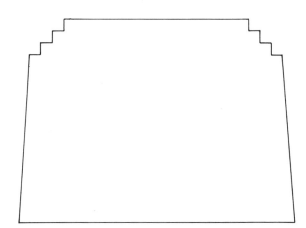

FRONT: Cast on 96 (102—108) sts. Work even in pattern for 3" (4"—5"). To divide for front opening, work to center, attach second ball of yarn and complete row. Working on both sides at once, work same as back until armholes measure 2¼" (2½"—2¾")—40 (42—43) sts on each side. Place center 10 sts of each side on holder. At each center edge, dec 1 st every row 12 (11—12) times. Bind off 6 (7—7) sts at beg of next 6 rows.

HOOD: Sew shoulder seams. Pick up and k 88 (84—88) sts around neckline, including sts on holders. Inc 14 (18—14) sts on next row, then work even in pattern for 10". Divide sts evenly on 2 needles and weave edges together.

FINISHING: Sew side, lower edge, and sleeve seams. Set in sleeves. Sew in zipper. With right side facing, work 1 row sc around hood edge. Crochet chain long enough to weave through sc edging to make tie. (Or use ribbon, if desired.)

33

SIMPLE FISHERMAN'S SWEATER

KIDS' SWEATERS • MEDIUM

I stayed away from cables for a long time. I thought they were difficult. But, like everything else in knitting and crocheting, they are not difficult at all. After half an hour or so of concentration and attention cabling becomes a smooth operation. Once you learn the technique, you can make bigger or smaller, more elaborate cables and combinations of cables, leading to one of those richly embossed creations that you'll treasure for years.

A PHOTOGRAPH OF THE SIMPLE FISHERMAN'S SWEATER APPEARS ON PAGE 4 OF THE COLOR SECTION.

Sizes: Children's small (medium—large).

Materials: Reynolds Unscoured Fisherman's Yarn, 6 (7—8) skeins. Knitting needles, #5 and #3. Four double-pointed knitting needles or circular knitting needle, #3. Cable needle.

Gauge: Stockinette stitch, 4 stitches = 1"; 5 rows = 1". One cable = 1".

Pattern (multiple of 11 stitches plus 10): Make Bobble (MB): In next st, (yo, k 1) 3 times, turn work around, sl 1, p 5, turn again, sl 1, k 5, turn again, (p 2 tog) 3 times, turn again, sl 1, k 2 tog, pass the slip stitch over the k 2 tog. Row 1: P 2, *sl 3 sts to cable needle and hold in front of work, k next 3 sts, k 3 sts from cable needle (one cable), p 2, MB, p 2, repeat from *, end work one cable, p 2. Row 2: K 2, *p 6, k 2, p 1 in back of st, k 2, repeat from *, end p 6, k 2. Row 3: P 2, *k 6, p 5, repeat from *, end k 6, p 2. Row 4: K 2, *p 6, k 5, repeat from *, end p 6, k 2. Row 5: Repeat row 3. Row 6: Repeat row 4. Row 7: Repeat row 3. Row 8: Repeat row 4.

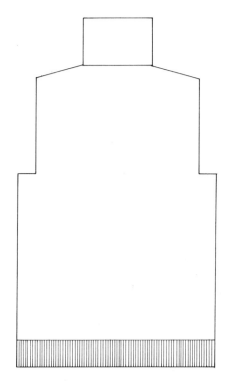

Working both sides at once, at each neck edge dec 1 st every other row 4 times—8 (10—12) sts on each side. Work even until armholes measure 4¾″ (5″—6¼″). Bind off 4 (5—6) sts at beg of next 4 rows.

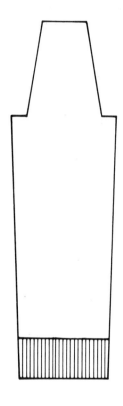

BACK: Cast on 54 (58—65) sts. Work k 1, p 1 ribbing for 2″. **Row 1:** P 0 (2—0) sts, work row 1 of pattern to last 0 (2—0) sts, p 0 (2—0). **Row 2:** K 0 (2—0) sts, work row 2 of pattern to last 0 (2—0) sts, k 0 (2—0). Continue in this manner, working first and last 0 (2—0) sts in reverse stockinette st, until piece measures 9½″ (11¼″—12¼″). Bind off 3 sts at beg of next 2 rows. Dec 1 st each end every other row 4 (4—5) times—40 (44—49) sts. Work even until armholes measure 4¾″ (5″—6¼″). Bind off 4 (5—6) sts at beg of next 4 rows. Sl remaining 24 (24—25) sts onto holder.

SLEEVES: Cast on 25 (27—29) sts. Work k 1, p 1 ribbing for 2″. **Row 1:** P 2 (3—4) sts, work row 1 of pattern to last 2 (3—4) sts, p 2 (3—4). **Row 2:** K 2 (3—4), work row 2 of pattern to last 2 (3—4) sts, k 2 (3—4). Continuing in this manner, inc 1 st each end every 1¼″ 6 (7—8) times—37 (41—45) sts. Work even until sleeve measures 11″ (13″—14″). Bind off 3 sts at beg of next 2 rows. Dec 1 st each end every other row 10 (11—12) times. Bind off remaining 11 (13—15) sts.

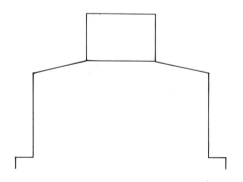

FRONT: Work same as back until armholes measure 2¾″ (3″—4¼″). Work across first 12 (14—16) sts, sl center 16 (16—17) sts onto a holder, attach second ball of yarn, work across remaining 12 (14—16) sts.

FINISHING: Sew left shoulder seam. Turtleneck: With right side facing and dp or circular needles, k 24 (24—25) sts from back holder, pick up and k 10 sts along left neck edge, k 16 (16—17) sts from front holder, pick up and k 10 sts along right neck edge—60 (60—62) sts. Work in k 1, p 1 ribbing for 4″. Bind off in ribbing. Sew right shoulder, underarm, and sleeve seams. Set in sleeves.

34

KID'S COWBOY JACKET

KIDS' SWEATERS • EASY

Not just for chronological kids, of course.

Sizes: Children's small (medium—large).

Materials: Bernhard Ullmann's 4-ply Knitting Worsted, 2 (3—4) skeins brown. Knitting needles, #8. Aluminum crochet hook, size J. 1—2 yards grosgrain ribbon. 5 ½" leather-covered buttons.

Gauge: 3½ stitches = 1"; 4½ rows = 1" (with yarn worked double).

Pattern: Stockinette stitch with V-shaped purled ridge on front and back.

PHOTOGRAPHS OF THE KID'S COWBOY JACKET APPEAR ON THE BACK COVER AND ON PAGES 6 AND 8 OF THE COLOR SECTION.

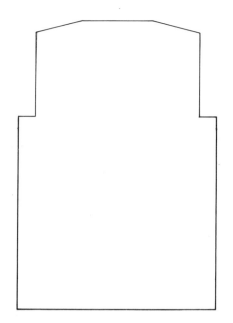

BACK: Cast on 44 (50—56) sts. Work even in stockinette st until piece measures 9½" (11"—12"). Bind off 2 (3—3) sts at beg of next 2 rows. Dec 1 st each end every other row 2 (2—3) times—36 (40—44) sts, ending with a wrong side row. To establish V-shaped reverse stockinette sts (into which fringes will be worked later): Next row: K 17 (19—21), p 2, k 17 (19—21). On next row and every following row, work sts on outer sides of reversed sts in previous row in reverse stockinette st (p on right side row, k on wrong side row) to form V. At the same time, work even until armholes measure 4¾" (5"—6¼"). Bind off 5 (6—7) sts at beg of next 4 rows. Bind off remaining 16 sts.

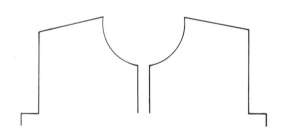

LEFT FRONT: Cast on 25 (28—31) sts. K 3 (front band), place marker on needle, k across. Working front band sts in garter st and remainder in stockinette st, work even until piece measures 9½" (11"—12"), ending at side edge. Bind off 2 (3—3) sts at beg of next row. Dec 1 st at same edge every other row 2 (2—3) times, ending with a wrong side row—21 (23—25) sts. To establish V-shaped reverse stockinette sts: Next row: K 17 (19—21), p 1, sl marker on needle, k 3. On next row and every following row, work next st toward arm edge in reverse stockinette st, and at the same time, work even

until armhole measures 1¾" (2"—3¼"), ending at front edge. Bind off 5 sts at beg of next row, then dec 1 st at same edge every other row 6 times, then work even until armhole measures 4¾" (5"—6¼"), ending at arm edge. Bind off 5 (6—7) sts at beg of next row. Work one row even. Bind off 5 (6—7) sts. Mark front edge for placement of 5 evenly spaced buttons.

RIGHT FRONT: Work same as left front, reversing all shaping and placement of V sts and working 5 buttonholes along front band as follows: K 1, bind off next st, k 1. On the following row, cast on 1 st over that bound off.

SLEEVES: Cast on 22 (24—24) sts. Working in stockinette st, inc 1 st each end every 1½" 5 (6—8) times—32 (36—40) sts. Work even until piece measures 11" (13"—14"). Bind off 2 (3—3) sts at beg of next 2 rows. Dec 1 st each end every other row 8 (9—10) times. Bind off remaining 12 (12—14) sts.

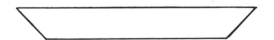

COLLAR: Cast on 32 sts. Working in stockinette st, inc 1 st each end every other row until piece measures 3". Bind off.

FINISHING: Block pieces. Sew shoulder, side, and sleeve seams. Set in sleeves. Cut 6" lengths of yarn for fringe. Using crochet hook, knot 1 fringe in each st on V's. Work 1 fringe in every other st along sleeve seams. Sew ribbon to wrong side of front bands, making slits for buttonholes. Sew on buttons.

35

A PONCHO EVEN A KID COULD KNIT

KIDS' SWEATERS • EASIEST

*"Hey, Ma, why don't you teach me to knit?"
All right, let the little cherub knit something
she (or he) can wear. This poncho fills the bill.
It's as easy to knit as a scarf, but it's not a
scarf. What it actually is is two scarves, seamed
as shown to make a poncho. The one pictured
in the section of color photographs was done
by an adult in her spare time in 5 days, but
with doubled yarn and bigger needles, even a
child with no spare time may be able to turn
one out over a weekend, in time to wear it to
school on Monday.*

*Because of its simplicity, it's an ideal base
for flights of fancy. Embroider scenes, flowers,
birds on the finished poncho; work a patch-
work of different knitting stitches; mix knitting and crocheting; create a crazy quilt of
different color stripes (a neat way to use up
old yarn scraps). For the first-time knitter,
this poncho is the best project.*

**A PHOTOGRAPH OF A PONCHO EVEN A KID COULD
KNIT APPEARS ON PAGE 4 OF THE COLOR SECTION.**

Sizes: Children's small (medium—large).

Materials: Spinnerin's Marvel-Twist Deluxe Knitting Worsted, 2 (3—4) skeins navy. Knitting needles,
#7.

Gauge: 4 stitches = 1"; 8 rows = 1".

Pattern: Garter stitch.